Melinda Haley

American Criminal Justice

Melinda Haley

American Criminal Justice

Just World Beliefs, Ethnicity, and Juror Bias

LAP LAMBERT Academic Publishing

Impressum/Imprint (nur für Deutschland/ only for Germany)
Bibliografische Information der Deutschen Nationalbibliothek: Die Deutsche Nationalbibliothek verzeichnet diese Publikation in der Deutschen Nationalbibliografie; detaillierte bibliografische Daten sind im Internet über http://dnb.d-nb.de abrufbar.

Coverbild: www.ingimage.com

Verlag: LAP LAMBERT Academic Publishing AG & Co. KG
Dudweiler Landstr. 99, 66123 Saarbrücken, Deutschland
Telefon +49 681 3720-310, Telefax +49 681 3720-3109
Email: info@lap-publishing.com

Herstellung in Deutschland:
Schaltungsdienst Lange o.H.G., Berlin
Books on Demand GmbH, Norderstedt
Reha GmbH, Saarbrücken
Amazon Distribution GmbH, Leipzig
ISBN: 978-3-8383-7342-3

Imprint (only for USA, GB)
Bibliographic information published by the Deutsche Nationalbibliothek: The Deutsche Nationalbibliothek lists this publication in the Deutsche Nationalbibliografie; detailed bibliographic data are available in the Internet at http://dnb.d-nb.de.

Cover image: www.ingimage.com

Publisher: LAP LAMBERT Academic Publishing AG & Co. KG
Dudweiler Landstr. 99, 66123 Saarbrücken, Germany
Phone +49 681 3720-310, Fax +49 681 3720-3109
Email: info@lap-publishing.com

Printed in the U.S.A.
Printed in the U.K. by (see last page)
ISBN: 978-3-8383-7342-3

DEDICATION

I would like to dedicate this book to my mother Sharon Rose Haley. Mom, your unwavering support, unconditional love, and positive regard significantly impacted my life. Your belief in me got me through all the rough times. Your financial and physical support was also very important; had you not provided my children with daycare so that I could go to school, I would still be working at Safeway. Thank you mom, I love you very much!

I would also like to dedicate this book to my husband Gary, my daughter Stephanie Rose, and my son Travis. This was a long and ardent process. I appreciate all your patience and support throughout the writing of this book. Each made sacrifices so that this work could be completed. Besides that, you are my world! I love you all very much!

In addition, I would like to dedicate this book to Dr. David Capuzzi who was my professor and department chair during my Master's program at Portland State University in Portland Oregon and who has continued to be a friend and mentor to me during my Ph.D. program. David, your encouragement and recognition of my abilities during my Master's program gave me the ability to dream of bigger things to come. Your advice and mentorship has been priceless. I can unequivocally say you have touched my life in positive ways and that I would not be where I am today without your guidance and support. I look forward to many years of continued friendship.

TABLE OF CONTENTS

CHAPTER ONE

Introduction

The current study was interested in how a juror's just world beliefs, his or her attitudes toward the punishment of criminals, his or her ethnicity, and the criminal defendant's ethnicity may relate to a juror's perceptions toward a criminal defendant, specifically in sentencing decisions. These factors are important because while the United States (U.S.) has only 5% of the world's population, it has 25% of the world's prisoners. As of 2005, 1 out of every 136 Americans were living behind bars with two-thirds of these prisoners composed of racial and ethnic minorities (Benson, 2003; Facts About Prisoners and Prisons, 2007; International Center For Prison Studies, 2007; Platt, 2001; Reducing Racial Disparity, 2007).

Since the 1980s, the state and federal prison population in this country has seen unprecedented growth and has increased by 400% - 600% (Bureau of Justice Statistics, 2002b, 2006; Facts about Prisoners and Prisons, 2007; Morgan, Beer, Fitzgerald, & Mandracchia, 2007; Platt, 2001). At the same time, because of overcrowding and punitive measures many jails and prisons have violated human rights conditions; so much so, that the United Nations Committee against Torture cited the U.S. for violations of the international treaty and the treatment of U.S. inmates has garnered the attention and disapproval of the international community (Olson, 2000). Currently, the U.S. has the highest prison incarceration rate in the world (Benson, 2003; Facts about Prisoners and Prisons, 2007; Platt, 2001). This chapter will give a brief overview of the study including the statement of the problem, a discussion on bias and racism, on models pertaining to bias and racism and bias against criminal defendants, the significance of the study, as well as providing conceptual definitions, the purpose of the study, and the research questions being addressed.

Statement of the Problem

The criminal justice system in the U.S. is not an equal opportunity system and racial disparity within this system is staggering (Bureau of Justice Statistics, 2002a, 2006; Davies, 2003; Luna, 2003; Reducing Racial Disparity, 2007; Sorensen, Hope, & Stemen, 2003). It is an unspoken assumption that the U.S. criminal justice system has been historically fraught with racism from its conception (Davies, 2003; Enomoto, 1999). Racial disparity within the justice system is said to exist whenever the proportion of minorities processed through the criminal justice system exceeds the proportion such groups represent in the general population (Davies, 2003; Reducing Racial Disparity, 2007). As of 1991, 66% of the inmates in U.S. prisons and jails were of minority status (Bureau of Justice Statistics, 2002a, 2006; Facts About Prisoners and Prisons, 2007; International Center for Prison Studies, 2007; Reducing Racial Disparity, 2007). As Platt (2001) so bluntly put it, "as South Africa moves closer to Western-style democracy, we are moving back to an apartheid system of justice" (p. 148). This racial disparity manifests itself in several of the criminal justice arenas, such as crime bias, sentencing bias, incarceration length bias, and juror bias.

Crime Bias

The ratio of contact with the criminal justice system from routine traffic stops to incarcerations between those of European American descent and minorities is severely disproportionate (Bureau of Justice Statistics, 2002a, 2006; Davies, 2003; Luna, 2003; Sorensen et al., 2003). One example of this inequality is the racial disparity among drug related offenders. African American and Hispanic American inmates represent 79% of the state prison population incarcerated for drug offenses: African American (56%) and Hispanic American (23%). These incarceration rates are well above their respective drug use rates: African American (13%) and Hispanic American (9%) (Drug Policy, 2007; King & Mauer, 2002).

Sentencing Bias

Discrimination can be considered throughout every level of the criminal justice system. For instance, there are different penalties for rich (predominantly European American) and poor (predominantly minority) drug users. Federal law distinguishes punishment differentially between the powder cocaine sold in rich neighborhoods and the crack cocaine sold in poor neighborhoods (Crack Cocaine, 1995; Drug Policy, 2007; Federal Crack Cocaine Sentencing, 2007; Glasser, 2000).

For example, a drug dealer selling five grams of crack cocaine (about the weight of two pennies) will receive a five year mandatory minimum sentence whereas the dealer selling powder cocaine would have to get caught selling 500 grams, or 100 times more than the crack dealer, to receive the same sentence (Coyle, 2002; Crack Cocaine, 1995; Drug Policy, 2007). Therefore, a drug dealer charged with trafficking 500 grams of powder cocaine, worth approximately $40,000, would receive a shorter sentence then a drug dealer selling crack cocaine worth $500 (Coyle; Crack Cocaine).

McDonald and Carlson (1993) found that African Americans and Hispanic Americans, when convicted of federal offenses and subjected to the provisions of the Sentencing Reform Act of 1984, were more likely than those of European Americans to be sentenced to prison. Another study conducted in 1996 by the National Reporting Program, found that European American felons were less likely than African American felons to be sent to prison. Only 32% of European Americans were given prison terms in comparison to 46% of African Americans (as cited in Levin, Langan, & Brown, 2000).

Incarceration Length Bias

When looking at sentencing length, African Americans received longer average prison sentences (71 months) than either European Americans (50 months), or Hispanic Americans (48 months) (Heaney, 1991). Heaney also found that European Americans are over three times more likely than African Americans to receive probation instead of incarceration for offenses involving drugs and violence. In a related study by Williams (1995), it was found that even when non-European Americans appealed prison terms found to be in excess of the recommended maximum sentencing guidelines, they were more likely than European Americans to have the trial court's decision affirmed after the appeal. However, other research does not show this disparity and find that sentencing between African Americans and European Americans are relatively comparable in incarceration length (Levin et al., 2000).

Jury Bias

Although the process of jury selection was designed to prevent bias, jury bias can and does occur (Brennan, 2006; Ertel, 2005; Farmer & Percorino, 2000; Hafemeister, 2000; Landwehr et al., 2002; Perdue, 2005; Pruitt, 2002; Turner, 1996; Walker, 2007). Safeguards are implied, but may be ineffectual. For example, attorneys for both sides can exercise a limited right to excuse potential jurors who might be biased during the voir dire process (Brennan, 2006; Ertel, 2005; Mauro, 2005). Voir dire "to speak the truth" is the process in which the defense and the prosecution can question potential jurors. During this process, lawyers can challenge a prospective juror "for cause" if that person says or otherwise expresses a bias against the attorney's case. However, this juror selection process is often in itself biased, as many attorneys will use stereotypical criteria to excuse potential jurors (Hafemeister, 2000; Jurand, 2003). For example, Hafemeister stated that attorneys often rely on group stereotypes such as that the poor are more empathic toward defendants than are the rich.

Potential jurors are not tabula rasa, but rather come with their own set of biases and opinions that influence the juror's decision-making (Ertel, 2005; Farmer & Pecorino, 2000; Landwehr et al., 2002; Perdue, 2005; Pruitt, 2002; Walker, 2007). Despite this acknowledgment, judges have few guidelines or instructions for determining juror bias (Brennan, 2006). Judges frequently make decisions on their own intuition on a case-by-case basis (Hafemeister, 2000).

The current study focused on select variables hypothesized to be related to juror bias. The first step in an inmate's incarceration begins with his or her arrest and subsequent trial. If jury members show bias toward the defendant based upon the juror's ethnicity, the defendant's ethnicity, the juror's attitude toward the punishment of criminals, or the juror's beliefs in a just world, then inmates in general, and minority inmates specifically, may be unjustly incarcerated.

Bias and Racism

The ethnic makeup of U.S. jails and prisons suggests that there is bias in the criminal justice system. Several models have been proposed to explain ethnic bias in general, and bias toward inmates specifically. These models and theories are not exclusive or exhaustive, but represent some of the major positions on bias toward these populations.

Models and Theories Pertaining to Ethnic Bias

The following models address ethnic bias: The culturally deficient model and scientific racism.

The Culturally Deficient Model. When a person or institution looks upon a part of its membership as culturally deficient because that culture is not a part of the majority European American culture, members are marginalized and held as less than worthy. According to

Hansman, Spencer, and Grant (1999) and Oppenheimer (2001), those cultures that are closest to Western ideals fare the best because they are perceived as less deficient than those more diverse from Western ideals.

Cultural contributions are discounted because they do not meet dominant Western standards. Therefore, these cultural contributions are perceived as deficient. A culture of power is established and the rules become a reflection of the culture that has power. Language, especially when used as racial slurs, reinforces that power, and continues to minimize and discount individuals based on color and culture (Mahar, 2001; Smith, 1999).

Scientific Racism (Genetic Deficient Model). Scientific racism posits that biological inheritance determines the character and behavior of social groups that have been classified into races (Barkan, 1992; Oppenheimer, 2001; Rutledge, 1995). Scientific racism promotes the concept that there is a hierarchy of races whereby some are superior and others inferior and these differences can be ascertained by the sciences (e.g., anthropological, psychological, and medical studies) (Jensen, 1967, 1969a, 1969b, 1969c, 1970, 1972; Oppenheimer, 2001).

Scientific racism espouses that genetic differences account for variables in certain abilities (e.g., IQ), and have been used as a foundation to deny certain groups opportunity, yet bestow onto others privilege (Holloway, 1999). Oppenheimer (2001) stated that within the racial taxonomy some immigrant groups were considered inferior to others depending on how different they were in mannerisms and skin color from European Americans. Therefore, the closer one is to looking and acting like a European American, the more acceptance and social status one can conceivably obtain.

Scientific racism has been used in the U.S. to justify the domination, subjugation, and genocide of other cultures by the European American majority (Barkan, 1992; Oppenheimer, 2001; Rutledge, 1995). For example, slavery was justified because African Americans were not thought to belong to the human race, nor capable of caring for themselves.

Models Pertaining to Bias Toward Criminal Offenders

In addition to theories and models that present explanations of ethnic bias so too are there models and theories that attempt to explain criminality and bias within the criminal justice system. Minority criminals or those accused, are doubly discriminated against, first for their criminal status and then again for their ethnic status. While many studies have documented bias within the criminal justice system there has not been a definitive answer found to account for the discrepancies between minority and majority individual incarceration rates or length. Several theories have been proposed, however no concrete explanation has been found regarding the inherent differences in treatment of persons from minority groups (e.g., African American, Hispanic American) in comparison to the majority ethnic group (e.g., European American) when looking at juror bias and how that affects sentence length.

Belief in a Just World

The theory of interest in the current study is the theory proposed by Lerner (1977, 1980), which states individuals have a fundamental belief in a just world. Belief in a just world can be described as a belief that bad things do not happen to good people, and people therefore, generally get what they deserve and deserve what they get. According to the Just World Theory developed by Lerner (1977, 1980), people have a basic need to believe in a just world. According to Lerner there are two primary means that people can use to maintain their just world beliefs when these beliefs are threatened, which is through behavior and attributes (Maes, 1998b).

For example, people with just world beliefs consider that certain behaviors deserve certain outcomes and when a person performs a bad act (e.g., robbing a bank), then he or she deserves an equally bad outcome (e.g. going to jail). In turn, when people perform a good act (e.g., giving to charity), they deserve equally good things to happen to them (e.g., winning the lottery). When a bad thing happens to a good person it upsets the balance. In order to achieve balance a person will either reassess the event or attribute the outcome as just by reinterpreting the behavior of the person. Equilibrium is also restored by devaluing the person in order to keep a sense of order that the world is a just place (Lerner, 1977, 1980).

Traditionally, this belief explains individual reactions to others who are less fortunate such as victims of crime or disease (Hafer & Olson, 1998; Lerner & Montada, 1998). When a person who maintains a belief that the world is a just place sees suffering then he or she experiences dissonance. If the world is just then how could an innocent person suffer? In order to reduce his or her own dissonance the person who believes that the world is just will attribute traits to the person suffering that would explain his or her fate (Hafer & Olson). If a person does not do this then his or her whole foundation can crumble and he or she may lose faith in the future. Therefore, to maintain the belief that the world is just despite contradictory evidence, the individual will blame the victim (Lerner, 1980; Lerner & Montada; Murray, Spadafore, & McIntosh, 2005).

The stronger an individual's belief that the world is just the more dissonance he or she will experience when witnessing contrary evidence and the more he or she will blame the victim for his or her circumstances. Therefore instead of changing his or her belief the individual will use cognitive strategies to make the victim's situation more deserved by attribution (Hafer & Olson, 1998; Lerner & Miller, 1978).

Significance of the Study

This research will contribute to the growing knowledge base regarding the treatment of minorities within the U.S. criminal justice system and the inherent ethnic bias apparent within. Research and current statistics indicate there is racial disparity within this system, yet no clear answers have emerged to explain this difference. As society in the U.S. becomes integrated culturally it is important to recognize the role discrimination plays in its justice system.

In looking at the personal attitudes and just world beliefs of university students, this research will essentially tap the attitudes and beliefs of future attorneys, advocates, judges, and jurors who play such a crucial role within this system. If research can identify attitudes and beliefs that are salient in contributing to bias within the criminal justice system changes can be made that might remediate this situation.

Relationship to Counseling Psychology

The profession of counseling psychology has long maintained its differential role in the mental health field as professionals enlisted to facilitate intrapersonal and interpersonal functioning and growth across the life span. The profession's focus has been on the utilization of individual, group, and community interventions for treatment of client needs, including but not limited to emotional, behavioral, vocational, and various mental health problems (Gelso & Fretz, 2001). Early on it was recognized that environmental and contextual factors shaped individual lives and contributed or detracted from the work psychologists did with clients (Goodman et al., 2004). It has also been recognized that at times it is necessary that counseling psychologists use the resources available to them to combat the social injustices suffered by their clients in order to help them (Goodman et al.; Kiselica & Robinson, 2001; Romero & Chan, 2005).

Social Justice and Social Advocacy

There has been an increasing push from the counseling psychology field to engage in social justice work (Baluch, Pieterse, & Bolden, 2004; Goodman et al., 2004; Romero & Chan, 2005). The social justice and social advocacy movement in counseling psychology requires that counseling psychologists also focus on environmental or extrapsychic forces that adversely affect the emotional and physical well-being of their clients (Kiselica & Robinson, 2001; Vera & Speight, 2003). Counseling psychologists can no longer be content to sit back and work with clients solely on intraphsyic concerns when the very environments these clients live in may be impacting these concerns (Kiselica & Robinson, 2001; Romero & Chan, 2005).

Counseling psychologists have over time come forth with many examples of scholarly or practical work that combated social injustice and sought changes at the societal, institutional, or political level in response to their interactions with clients and humanity (Beers, 1908; Calkins, 1995; Crawford, 2003; Goodman et al., 2004; Kiselica & Robinson, 2001; Tomes, 2004).

- In 2001, the Fourth National Counseling Psychology Conference in Houston called for an agenda of social justice in terms of research, practice, and training focusing on social justice issues (Goodman et al., 2004). When looking at multicultural competence among counseling psychologists it has been said that true multicultural competence cannot be achieved without a corresponding commitment to social justice and social advocacy (Goodman et al., 2004; Vera & Speight, 2003).

Social justice work can be done on many levels:

- Micro: Includes working with individuals and families
- Meso: Includes working with communities and organizations
- Macro: Includes working with social structures, ideologies, and polices (Goodman et al., 2004).

Counseling psychologists work as advocates when they plead on behalf of a client, a group, or a social cause. Counseling psychologists who act as social advocates work within the social contexts in which their client problems occur. They also take action to eliminate or reduce social problems. This could be working on such problems as poverty, unequal access to opportunities, and various forms of prejudice, which adversely affect clients (Kiselica & Robinson, 2001). It is important for counseling psychologists to challenge “institutional and social barriers that impede academic, career, personal, or social development” (Kiselica & Robinson, p. 387). Kiselica and Robinson strongly suggest that it is a counselor or psychologist’s responsibility to “use all the methods of counseling and psychotherapy to confront injustice and inequality in society” (p. 387).

One aspect of social justice or advocacy work pertains to changing systems that perpetuate bias and racism toward ethnic minorities. According to Goodman and colleagues (2004) this would constitute a macro level of advocacy work to impact social structures, ideologies, and polices. Racism and bias exist in many arenas and the criminal justice system is just one of many. However, the taking of an individual’s freedom is a very serious undertaking and can present a lasting stigma, which can affect that individual’s growth. For example, the stigma of being a former inmate is pervasive and can affect the rest of that individual’s life in many negative ways (Allard, 2002; Mauer, 2001, 2003; Mauer & Chesney-Lind, 2003).

An individual whose daily life consists of racism and prejudice can be considered handicapped against his or her will (Goodman et al., 2004). The individual may face extensive barriers in the way of fulfilling his or her own intrapersonal and interpersonal growth. Prejudicial reactions can severely limit a minority individual from achieving his or her optimal success in meeting emotional, behavioral, and vocational goals, which can severely limit the individual’s ability to realize socioeconomic, educational, and vocational aspirations (Kiselica & Robinson, 2001). As counseling psychology becomes more congruent with the concepts of multiculturalism and social justice, it is imperative that counseling psychologists contribute to research that will aid in the remediation, prevention, and knowledge of what creates racism and bias.

Helms (as cited in Goodman et al., 2004) has made explicit that counseling psychologists need to make racism a focus of their call for social advocacy and social justice, because multiculturalism and broader definitions of culture have shifted the field’s focus from systemic structures that recreate hierarchies. Certainly, research has shown that bias and racism within the criminal justice system has treated people of color unfairly. Therefore, "unless fundamental change occurs within our neighborhoods, schools, media, culture, and religious, political, and social institutions, our work with individuals is destined to be, at best, only partially successful" (Goodman et al., p. 6).

Based on the tenets of the social justice movement within counseling psychology, the current study seeks to contribute to the research base at the macro level and continue to build awareness regarding the treatment of ethnic minorities within the U.S. criminal justice system. This study explores the relationships between a juror's just world beliefs, his or her attitudes toward the punishment of criminals, his or her ethnicity, and the ethnicity of the criminal defendant to sentencing decisions. This research explores the phenomenon reflected in the Bureau of Justice Statistics that ethnic minorities receive longer sentences for the same commission of crimes than European Americans (Bureau of Justice Statistics, 2006).

Conceptual and Operational Definitions

The following terms are defined in order to ensure that all readers have the same conceptions as the researcher.

Bias. Bias occurs when a person has a prejudiced outlook or unreasoned judgment based on some type of criteria (e.g., ethnicity, socioeconomic status, sexual orientation) (Webster, 1993). For the purpose of this study, bias was operationally defined as the participant's score on the Attitudes Toward the Punishment of Criminals scale and the participant's choice for sentencing on the Juror Decision Record.

African Americans. African Americans are individuals classified as being of the Negroid race whose ancestors, usually in predominant part, were indigenous to Sub-Saharan Africa (Webster, 1993). For the purpose of this study, African American ethnicity was operationally defined as the ethnicity listed on the arrest card.

European Americans. European Americans are individuals of European decent, classified as being of the Caucasoid (European American) race, and who are non-Hispanic American (Webster, 1993). For the purpose of this study, European American ethnicity was operationally defined as the participant's self-selection as indicated on the demographic sheet and as the ethnicity listed on the arrest card.

Cultural Racism. Hansman et al., (1999) defined cultural racism as "when power of the majority group, plus their racial prejudice, results in the exclusions of cultural contributions of historically oppressed groups from textbooks, art, language, and music" (p. 2).

Ethnicity. Ethnicity is often confused with race, but ethnicity transcends beyond visible group membership and includes sociohistorical and sociopolitical experiences that explain why groups of individuals consider themselves to be a distinct people. Ethnicity refers to a shared worldview, language, and set of behaviors that are associated with a cultural heritage (Holcomb-McCoy, 2005).

Hispanic Americans. Hispanic Americans are individuals of the Caucasoid race and are of Latin American descent (Webster, 1993). For the purpose of this study, Hispanic American ethnicity was operationally defined as the participant's self-selection as indicated on the demographic sheet and as the ethnicity listed on the arrest card.

Jail. Jail is usually a county or city institution and persons are incarcerated there for up to one year.

Just world beliefs. Lerner (1977, 1980) defines just world beliefs as an individual's conviction that bad things do not happen to good people and that people generally get what they deserve and deserve what they get. For the purpose of this study, just world beliefs were operationally defined as the participant's score on the Just World Beliefs scale.

Mock Juror. A mock juror is a pseudo juror that is used by lawyers or researchers in a simulated trial (Bronson, 1987). For the purposes of this study a mock juror was operationally defined as the participant who independently reads the criminal case, deliberates on the information, and fills out the juror decision record.

Prison. Prisons are either state or federal institutions and individuals can be incarcerated there for more than one year and up to life.

Race. There is much controversy regarding the definition of race and ethnicity. Some report that race is a social construction that evolves based on political, social, and economic conditions (Ogletree, 2006). Some research, such as the International Haplotype Map (HapMap) Project correlates race with genetics and ancestry (Jones, 2006). The Food and Drug Administration (FDA), and other federal agencies, recognize five ethnicities (1) American Indian or Alaska Native, (2) Asian, (3) Black or African American, (4) Native Hawaiian or Other Pacific Islander, and (5) White. Furthermore the race of White is broken down into two ethnicities: Hispanic American or non-Hispanic American (Jones). For the purposes of this study the FDA's recognition of ethnicity as a member of one of the five above groups was accepted. Furthermore, Non- Hispanic American Whites were defined in this study as European American and Hispanic American Whites were referred to simply as Hispanic Americans.

Racism. Racism is a belief that race is the primary determinant of human traits, abilities, and capacities, and that racial differences determine the superiority of one race over another (Webster, 1993).

Racial Prejudice. Racial prejudice is defined as the "prejudgment by others that the members of a race are in some way inferior, dangerous, or repugnant" to members of groups that typically enjoy power and privilege (Campbell & Marable, 1996, p. 49).

Sentencing. A conclusion given on request or reached after deliberation (Webster, 1993). For the purposes of this study, sentencing was operationally defined as the choice of sentence length chosen by individual mock jurors on the juror decision record.

Purpose of the Study

The purpose of this study was to ascertain whether a potential juror's belief in a just world, his or her attitude toward the punishment of criminals, the ethnicity of the defendant, and the ethnicity of the juror, has a relationship to juror bias. In this study, the existence of discriminatory beliefs was assessed in a sample of university students composed of graduates and undergraduates. The current study looked at the beliefs and attitudes of students representing the ethnicities of European American and Hispanic American. The participants acted as mock jurors.

A more definitive explanation to the question of why more minorities are incarcerated and often receive longer sentences than many European Americans for the same crime may be answered by this study. This study looked at potential juror's Just World Beliefs, Attitudes Toward the Punishment of Criminals, ethnicity of the juror, and ethnicity of the defendant, to determine what relationship these variables had to sentence length and juror bias toward a criminal defendant.

Research Questions

The current study hypothesized that just world beliefs can be related to punitive attitudes toward defendants in a jury trial, because in order to keep the belief that the world is "just," a jury member must attribute what has happened to the defendant as being what he or she "deserves." In other words, an innocent person would not be accused of a crime and therefore the defendant must be guilty. Some research indicates a minority juror might be harsher in judgment on a defendant of his or her own ethnicity due to possible cultural factors such as being members of a collectivist society and feeling that the accused has let down the group (King, 1993; Miller & Hewitt, 1978). However, other research implies that a minority juror who is the same ethnicity as the defendant might be more lenient in the sentencing of that defendant. This is thought to be due to the shared experiences of ethnic bias and from the psychological need to maintain a positive self-image (Broeder, 1959; Crocker, Luhtanen, Blaine, & Broadnax 1994; Dane & Wrightsman, 1982; Enomoto, 1999; Johnson et al., 2002; King, 1993; Montada, 1998; Murray, Kaiser, & Taylor, 1997; Sellers, Smith, Shelton, Rowley, & Chaovous, 1998; Smith, 1991; Valk & Karu, 2001; Verkuyten, 2003; Wuensch, Campbell, Kesler, & Moore, 2002; Yueh-Ting & Ottati, 2002).

When one finds continual prejudice that hinders his or her ability to achieve success in areas of socioeconomic status, educational opportunity, and/or employment, and whose ethnic group is severely over-represented in the criminal justice system, it seems reasonable that he or she would probably not believe that the world is just (Furnham & Proctor, 1989; O'Quinn & Vogler, 1989). When considering just world theory it seems probable that individuals of ethnic minority groups would have lower just world beliefs then those individuals of the majority European American group due to ethnic experiences of racism.

It seems just as logical based upon the tenets of Scientific Racism, (also known as the Genetically Deficient Model) that African Americans would have lower just world beliefs than Hispanic Americans due to phenotypal characteristics because Hispanic Americans more closely resemble European Americans in skin color than do African Americans. The theory of Scientific Racism suggests that the closer one is to looking and acting like a European American Anglo-Saxon the more acceptance and social status one can conceivably obtain. Therefore, even though there may be more language differences between Hispanic Americans and European Americans than there are between European Americans and African

Americans, theoretically, Hispanic Americans should not experience as much racism and prejudice as do African Americans, because of being more similar in phenotypal characteristics to European Americans (Oppenheimer, 2001). Criminal justice statistics confirm that Hispanic Americans have lower incarceration rates and sentence lengths than do African Americans (Bureau of Justice Statistics, 2002c, 2002e, 2006; Facts About Prisoners and Prisons, 2007; Platt, 2001).

The following general research questions are set forth:

- Is there a difference between ethnicities regarding beliefs that the world is just?
- Is there a difference between ethnicities regarding attitudes toward the punishment of criminals?
- Is the ethnicity of the juror related to his or her sentencing decisions when the criminal defendant is of the same, or of a different ethnicity, than the juror?
- What role does the ethnicity of the juror, ethnicity of the defendant, and the juror's just world beliefs play in juror bias?
- Is there a relationship between the juror's just world beliefs and his or her sentencing decisions regarding a criminal defendant?
- Is there a relationship between a juror's just world beliefs and he or her attitudes toward the punishment of criminals?
- Is there a relationship between a juror's attitudes toward the punishment of criminals and his or her recommended sentence length for a criminal defendant?

Summary

Many studies and current statistics suggest that ethnic bias does exist within the criminal justice system. Theories have been postulated explaining why this might occur, but no comprehensive or satisfactory explanation has been found. One theory that has not been explored in relationship to juror bias toward criminal defendants is the theory of just world beliefs.

Just world beliefs are thought to be fundamental to cultural beliefs and worldview. If the world is just, then bad things do not happen to good people, and people deserve what they get and get what they deserve. According to just world belief theory if a juror has a high belief in a just world he or she would not be sympathetic to a defendant. In a just world innocent people are not accused of crimes they did not commit. Therefore, the juror holding this view would probably be biased against the defendant. Very little research has studied the just world beliefs of jurors, especially in combination with the ethnicity of juror and criminal defendant, in determination of juror bias.

Victim studies in civil trials indicate that jurors with high just world beliefs tend to blame the victim for his or her misfortune. While many studies have looked at ethnicity and just world beliefs in the jury decision-making process in civil trials few have looked at these variables in relationship to jury bias toward criminal offenders (Finamore & Carlson, 1987; Lambert & Raichle, 2000; Lerner, 1980; O'Quin & Vogler, 1989; Rubin & Peplau, 1975).

The current study looked at the relationship between the ethnicity of the juror, the ethnicity of the defendant, the juror's attitudes toward the punishment of criminals, and the juror's just world beliefs in relationship to juror bias as measured through the Attitudes Toward the Punishment of Criminals scale and Juror Sentencing Record.

While chapter one has given a brief overview of this study, chapter two provides more specific information on the different types of bias that can impact a juror's perceptions of a criminal defendant. Chapter two includes a discussion on the different models pertaining to ethnic bias and bias toward criminal defendants; how belief in a just world might impact juror perception, and how cultural factors might affect bias toward minority defendants.

Chapter three provides a description of the design of this study, sampling procedures, and research hypotheses. Chapter three also provides a discussion of the instruments used, which were The Just World Belief Scale (Rubin & Peplau, 1975) and the Attitudes Toward the Punishment of Criminals Scale (Wang & Thurstone, 1931 as cited in Shaw & Wright, 1967).

Chapter four presents the results of the seven hypotheses, none of which were found significant, while chapter five presents a discussion regarding the limitations of the study and the relevance of the findings.

CHAPTER TWO
Literature Review

The treatment of U.S. inmates has garnered the attention and disapproval of the international community (Olson, 2000; Platt, 2001). As of 2007, the U.S. had the highest prison incarceration rate in the world and while the U.S. has only 5% of the world's population, it has 25% of the world's prisoners (See table 1) (Facts About Prisoners and Prisons, 2007; Platt, 2001). As of 2005, 1 out of every 136 Americans was living behind bars with two-thirds of these prisoners composed of racial and ethnic minorities (Benson, 2003; Facts About Prisoners and Prisons, 2007; Platt, 2001; International Center For Prison Studies, 2007; Reducing Racial Disparity, 2007).

Table 1

Number of Prisoners in Different Countries

Country	Number of Prisoners
United States	2,193,798
China	1,548,498
Russian Federation	871,693
Mexico	213,152
United Kingdom	79,627
Canada	34,096

Note. International Center For Prison Studies, 2007.

Since the 1980s, the state and federal prison population in the U.S. has seen unprecedented growth, increasing by 400% - 600% (Bureau of Justice Statistics, 2002d, 2006; Facts About Prisoners and Prisons, 2007; Morgan et al., 2007; Platt, 2001) and despite falling crime rates since 1991, the rate of incarceration in U.S. prisons has increased by more than

50% (New Incarceration Figures, 2006). At the same time, because of overcrowding and punitive measures many jails and prisons have violated human rights conditions, so much so, that the United Nations Committee Against Torture cited the U.S. for violations of the international treaty (Olson, 2000).

It is an unspoken assumption that the U.S. criminal justice system has been historically fraught with racism from its conception and racial disparity within the U.S. criminal justice system is a recognized phenomenon (Bureau of Justice Statistics, 2002b, 2006; Davies, 2003; Luna, 2003; Reducing Racial Disparity, 2007; Sorensen et al., 2003). Racial disparity within the justice system is said to exist whenever the proportion of minorities processed through the criminal justice system exceeds the proportion such groups represented in the general population (Davies; Reducing Racial Disparity).

As of 2005, 66% of the inmates in U.S. prisons and jails were of minority status (Bureau of Justice Statistics, 2006). As Platt (2001) so bluntly put it, "as South Africa moves closer to Western-style democracy, we are moving back to an apartheid system of justice" (p. 148). Incarceration rates are so high for African American males, it is estimated that for every African American male who graduates from college, one hundred will be arrested (Platt). Current estimates are that 28% of African American males will be incarcerated at some point during their lifetime and currently African Americans make up 46% of the prison population (Bureau of Justice Statistics, 2002c, 2002e, 2006; Facts About Prisoners and Prisons, 2007).

These statistics are paralleled in many ways for Hispanic Americans in the Southwest and for Native Americans in states with a high Native American population (Platt, 2001). Current statistics for Hispanic Americans show that 16% of Hispanic American men will be incarcerated at some point in their lives and currently make up 4% of the inmate population. In comparison, the figure for European American males is only 4% and 2% respectively (Bureau of Justice Statistics, 2002e, 2006; Facts About Prisoners and Prisons, 2007). The number of Native Americans confined within U.S. state and federal prisons is 38% above the national average and the rate of incarceration of Native Americans in U.S. county jails is more than four times the national average, yet Native Americans make up less than 1% of the U.S. population (See table 2) (Greenfield & Smith, 1999).

Empirical data regarding whether there is racial disparity within the criminal justice system in terms of sentencing and length of incarceration are often controversial and dependent upon the type of crime and the state in which the crime was committed. However, the majority of research supports the notion that minorities are given longer and harsher sentences than European Americans for the same type of crime (Landwehr et al., 2002). This has been found true even though European Americans and ethnic minorities have essentially the same crime commission and recidivism rates (Alvarez & Bachman, 1996; Camp, 1994; Crawford, 2000; Free, 1997; Gastwirth & Nayak, 1997; Glasser, 2000; New York Study, 1996; Petersilia, 1983; Spohn & Holleran, 2000; Steffensmeier & Demuth, 2001).

Table 2

2006 Projected Incarceration Rate for Different Ethnic Groups

Ethnicity	Rate in Minority Pop.	% of US pop. From 2005 census
African American	1 out of 8	12.8%
Hispanic American	1 out of 26	14.4%
European American	1 out of 59	66.9%

Note. Criminal Offender Statistics, 2006; Facts About Prisoners and Prisons, 2006; U.S. Census Bureau Quick Facts, 2005.

This chapter provides more specific information on the different types of bias that can impact a juror's perceptions of a criminal defendant and includes a discussion on the different models pertaining to ethnic bias and bias toward criminal defendants, how belief in a just world might impact juror perception, and how cultural factors might affect bias toward minority defendants. This chapter also gives a brief overview of the different instruments used to measure just world beliefs and attitudes toward the punishment of criminals. In addition, a brief discussion regarding the implications of the literature is provided.

Crime Bias

The ratio of contact with the criminal justice system from routine traffic stops to incarcerations between European Americans and minorities is severely disproportionate

(Bureau of Justice Statistics, 2002b, 2006; Davies, 2003; Glasser, 2000; Luna, 2003; Sorensen et al., 2003). For example, the Bureau of Justice Statistics initiated the Survey of Police-Public Contact in 1999 (Schmitt, Langan, & Durose, 2002). The survey polled 80,543 U.S. residents who were 16 years or older about any face-to-face police contact they might have had in 1999. The survey found that 1 out of every 5 Americans had face-to-face police contact with the most frequent occurrence (52%) being a routine traffic stop (Schmitt et al.).

Of those with police contact, African Americans represented 17% of those pulled over, Hispanic Americans 16%, and European Americans 20%. According to this survey, European Americans had a greater probability of being pulled over in a routine traffic stop than either African Americans or Hispanic Americans. However, when the percentage of African Americans and Hispanic Americans were compared to the total percentage of the population, the average number of stops was greater for African American males (3%) than European American males (2%) and Hispanic American males (2%). Both African Americans (74%) and Hispanic Americans (82%) were less likely than European Americans (86%) to feel they were stopped legitimately (Schmitt et al., 2002).

Differences were also found for drivers stopped or ticketed for speeding. African Americans (76%) and Hispanic Americans (80%) were more likely than European Americans (67%) to be ticketed (Schmitt et al.). Furthermore, police were more likely to conduct a search of a vehicle belonging to an African American male (16%), or Hispanic American male (14%), than for a European American male (8%) (Schmitt et al.). This data shows that for those polled in this survey African American and Hispanic American males had their cars searched over twice as often as European American males.

In addition to racial disparity in routine traffic stops, a large percentage of minorities are incarcerated for a substance abuse issue. Since the 1980s, the number of inmates in U.S. jails and prisons who are incarcerated solely for a drug offense has grown by 1000% from 40,000 in 1980, to 453,000 by 1999. This is true even though 58% of the drug offenders have no history of violence and are not engaged in high-level drug activity (King & Mauer, 2002).

Just as with the general prison/jail population, there is also racial disparity among drug related offenders. Ethnic minorities represent 79% of the inmate population incarcerated in U.S. State and Federal prisons for drug offenses: African Americans (56%) and Hispanic Americans (23%). These incarceration rates are well above their respective drug use rates:

African Americans (13%) and Hispanic Americans (9%) (Drug Policy, 2007; King & Mauer, 2002).

In a report published by Alcoholism and Drug Abuse Weekly it was found that in Seattle from 1999-2001, African Americans were disproportionately arrested for selling cocaine at a ratio of 2:4. African Americans were 22.6 times more likely to be arrested for selling heroin and 31.6 times more likely to be arrested for selling methamphetamines than were European Americans. This was found true even though European Americans comprised a higher proportion of the people selling drugs (Report Finds, 2003).

These incarceration and arrest rates fluctuate by state. In some states, the numbers are much higher. For example in the state of Maryland during 1996-2001, 81% of inmates sentenced for a drug offense were African American (King & Mauer, 2002). Many studies indicate that European Americans are the most frequent users of illegal drugs (74%), but suffer a lower rate of negative consequences from use with incarceration rates of less than 20% (Bachman et al., 1991; Finch, 2001; Gillmore et al., 1990; King & Mauer, 2002).

Therefore, incarceration rates for drug offenses seem to fall disproportionately upon minority users. In some poor minority neighborhoods incarceration is not seen as something that could happen, but rather as an expected phase of life (Cose, 1999; Drug Policy, 2001; Matthews, 2000). Statistics indicate that 50% of minority men from the Watts area of Los Angles have been, or are, currently incarcerated and police discrimination towards ethnic minorities is a well-documented theme (Luna, 2003).

Sentencing Bias

Discrimination appears throughout every level of the criminal justice system. There even seems to be different penalties for rich (predominantly European American) and poor (predominantly ethnic minority) drug users. This is seen most clearly in the legal penalties for possession of crack cocaine versus that of powder cocaine (Cose, 1999; Lillie-Blanton, Anthony, & Schuster, 1993; Luna, 2003).

Crack cocaine and powder cocaine have the same chemical composition, psychotropic, and physiological effects (Crack Cocaine, 1995; Glasser, 2000). However, crack cocaine is sold in less expensive quantities and in lower-income neighborhoods. Federal law distinguishes the punishment of crack cocaine differentially from the powder cocaine sold in rich neighborhoods.

For example, a drug dealer convicted of selling five grams of crack cocaine (about the weight of two pennies) will receive a five-year mandatory minimum sentence. However, the drug dealer selling powder cocaine would have to get caught selling 500 grams (the weight of 200 pennies) than the crack dealer to receive the same sentence under current law and sentencing guidelines (Coyle, 2002; Crack Cocaine, 1995; Drug Policy, 2001; Free, 1997). Therefore, a drug dealer charged with trafficking 400 grams of powder cocaine worth approximately $40,000 would receive a shorter sentence then than a dealer selling crack cocaine worth $500 (Coyle; Crack Cocaine).

Crack cocaine is also the only drug that carries a mandatory minimum 5-year sentence for a first offence for possession; whereas possession of powder cocaine carries no minimum sentence and first time offenders usually get probation (Crack Cocaine, 1995). Statistics show that Hispanic Americans and European Americans are the majority users of crack cocaine, yet in 1999, 85% of all of those arrested and sentenced in federal court for the sale or use of crack cocaine were African American (Drug Policy, 2007).

A study conducted by McDonald and Carlson (1993) found that even when European American powder cocaine users were caught with the same amount of the drug as crack cocaine users African American sentences were 30% longer than European American sentences. The disparity in sentencing between these two classes of cocaine has meant that more ethnic minorities are arrested and serve longer sentences than do European Americans who use the same drug albeit in a different form. Similar analyses were found when comparing European American heroin users to ethnic minority heroin users. Using the sentencing guidelines 92% of all European Americans convicted for heroin distribution were given sentences toward the bottom of the sentencing guideline range whereas this occurred for only 83% of Hispanic Americans and 57% of African Americans (U.S. Sentencing Commission, 1991).

Other disparities between substances used and legal penalties can occur. When looking at the extent of damage alcohol can cause and its legal consequences as compared to illegal substance use, it is worth noting that drunk drivers are responsible for an estimated 22,000 deaths each year, while overall alcohol related deaths are deemed at 94,000 (Glasser, 2000).

In comparison, drug related deaths are estimated at only 21,000 (Does the Punishment Fit the Crime, 1993).

However, those convicted of a drug crime are disproportionately of low-income, minority status, and generally receive felony penalties with incarceration while the majority of drunk drivers are European American and are generally charged with a misdemeanor or sentences involving fines, license suspension, and community service (Does the Punishment Fit the Crime, 1993; Glasser, 2000). In addition even after arrest for the same offense, the length of sentencing is different between European Americans and minorities. For example, an African American juvenile who is convicted for a first time drug offense is 48 times more likely to go to juvenile prison then a European American juvenile. The average sentence length for the same crime also differs substantially: European Americans get 144 days, African Americans get 235 days, and Hispanic Americans get 306 days (Glasser, 2000; Matthews, 2000).

McDonald and Carlson (1993) found that African Americans and Hispanic Americans, when convicted of federal offenses and subject to the provisions of the Sentencing Reform Act of 1984, were more likely than European Americans to be sentenced to prison. Another study conducted in 1996 by the National Reporting Program confirmed that European Americans were less likely than African Americans to be sent to prison. For example, only 32% of European Americans were given prison terms in comparison to 46% of African Americans (Levin et al., 2000).

Unnever, Frazier, and Henretta, (1980) also conducted a study looking at racial differences in criminal sentencing. Data were collected from 90% of the pre-sentence investigative reports filed in one judicial district composed of six counties in Florida. The data represented information provided by 16 different probation officers and nine judges. The researchers coded information on variables into pre-established categories (e.g., ethnicity, sex, employment, and education level of the defendant).

A logit model was used to estimate the relationship of the different variables. The results of this study indicated that ethnicity had a moderately strong relationship to sentencing. When calculating the number of African Americans that received probation in comparison to European Americans, and when taking into consideration prior criminal record, European Americans received probation 2.3 times more often than did African Americans.

The authors noted that while defendant ethnicity was significant the standard error was large. Therefore, the actual ratio of European Americans to African Americans regarding probation could fall anywhere from 1.1 to 4.8. However, the authors also stated that European Americans had an 18% greater chance in the predicted probability of receiving probation than did African Americans when all other variables in the study were held constant.

This study did not determine that ethnicity alone influenced sentencing decisions as many other variables outside of ethnicity were looked at and many other variables were not. It may very well be that ethnicity, in combination with other variables (e.g., unemployment, age, education) did play a role. In fact, the authors did find significance regarding the variable of age. They found that each year of a defendant's age was associated with a predicted change in the odds ratio regarding probation or incarceration. They also found a similar correlation with the variable of prior arrests.

Incarceration Length Bias

When looking at sentencing length, African Americans received longer average prison sentences (71 months) than either European Americans (50 months) or Hispanic Americans (48 months) (Heaney, 1991). Heaney also found that European Americans are over three times more likely than African Americans to receive probation-only for offenses involving drugs and violence. In a related study by Williams (1995), it was found that even when minorities who had been sentenced in excess of the recommended maximum sentence appealed their sentences they were more likely than European Americans to have their appeal denied. However, other research did not find this disparity, but found sentences were comparable, at least between African Americans and European Americans (Levin et al., 2000).

Mazella and Feingold (1994) conducted a meta-analysis, which included 29 experimental studies looking at the relationship of race on recommended verdicts, guilt ratings, and recommended sentences. The analysis indicated that African Americans received longer sentences than European Americans when the crime was homicide or rape, but that European Americans received longer sentences than African Americans, when the crime was fraud.

Gordon, Bindrim, McNicholas, and Walden (1988) and Gordon (1990) found similar results. They found that African American burglars received longer sentences than European Americans, but European American embezzlers received longer sentences than African

Americans. Many such studies have indicated a pattern that defendants may receive longer sentences when they are convicted of crimes that are stereotypically associated with their ethnicity. Other research supports this finding (Bodenhausen, 2005; Bodenhausen & Wyer, 1985; Hurwitz & Peffley, 1997; Wuensch et al., 2002).

Racial disparity in the U.S. criminal justice system has existed since its inception (Davies, 2003). This disparity poses a problem at every stage of the system and has a snowball effect. For example, if bail practices result in similarly situated minorities being detained before trial at greater rates than European Americans, these minorities will also be disadvantaged at trial and sentencing by having less access to defense counsel, community resources, and treatment options (Reducing Racial Disparity, 2007). This disparity compromises the very principle of the U.S. criminal justice system, which was founded upon equality under the law.

Jury Bias

Although the process of jury selection was designed to prevent bias, jury bias can and does occur (Brennan, 2006; Ertel, 2005; Farmer & Percorino, 2000; Hafemeister, 2000; Landwehr et al., 2002; Perdue, 2005; Pruitt, 2002; Turner, 1996; Walker, 2007). Minimal safeguards have been emplaced. For example, attorneys for both the defense and prosecution can exercise a limited right to excuse potential jurors who might be biased during the voir dire process (Brennan, 2006; Ertel, 2005; Mauro, 2005; Perdue, 2005). Often this juror selection process in itself is biased as many attorneys use stereotypical criteria to excuse potential jurors (Bodenhausen & Wyer, 1985; Hafemeister, 2000). For example, Hafemeister stated that attorneys often rely on group stereotypes such as that the poor are more empathic toward defendants than are the rich, to eliminate potential jurors.

Steps to correct this practice by the U.S. Supreme Court have had minimal impact. Supreme Court rulings have made preemptory challenges to juror selection based upon race, ethnicity, and sex impermissible (Hafemeister, 2000; Mauro, 2005). Other challenges however have not yet been won. As of 2000, jurors could still be dismissed from serving on a jury based upon their language, culture, or religion (Hafemeister; Jurand, 2003) and as of 2001, jury pools were still disproportionately white, older, and wealthier than the overall population (Jurand, 2001).

It is recognized that potential jurors are not tabula rasa, but rather come with their own set of biases and opinions that influence the juror's decision-making (Ertel, 2005; Farmer & Pecorino, 2000; Landwehr et al., 2002; Pruitt, 2002; Perdue, 2005; Walker, 2007). Even though this is recognized, judges are given few guidelines or instructions for determining juror bias (Brennan, 2006). Decisions are often made on a case-by-case basis and the judge often relies heavily on his or her intuition (Hafemeister, 2000).

Often a potential jurist is asked whether he or she can set aside his or her bias and be impartial. There may be many reasons as to why a juror answers "yes" or "no" to this question, such as societal expectations, wanting to get out of jury duty, or wanting to influence the trial outcome. These issues are important because juror bias can affect trial outcomes (Brennan, 2006; Farmer & Pecorino, 2000; Turner, 1996; Walker, 2007).

Many professionals who practice as jury consultants, or scientific jury selection specialists, believe that juries can be swayed to give a verdict that is desired to either the prosecution or the defense (Enomoto, 1999; Moran, Cutler, & De Lisa, 1994; Pruitt, 2002; Strier & Shestowsky, 1999). If these claims are true, then trial by jury is significantly impacted by bias and persuasion. The practice of using jury consultants for jury selection began in 1971 with the famous trial of the Harrisburg 7, which was a trial of Vietnam draft resisters (Moran et al.; Strier & Shestowsky). This trial and other political trials like it (e.g., Camden 28, Gainesville eight, Wounded Knee, or Attica), led to the formation of an official organization called the National Jury Project (Moran et al.), which studies the impact jury selection procedures has on trials.

Jury specialists attempt to link demographic and personality traits to juror predispositions and then suggest case presentation based upon what would appeal to particular juror traits (Moran et al., 1994; Strier & Shestowsky, 1999). Everything is evaluated by these jury specialists, even the small details, such as the appearance and speaking style of the defendant and witnesses. These variables can then be manipulated to be pleasing to the jury with the hoped for result of a favorable outcome for whoever hired the consultants (Strier & Shestowsky).

As can be expected, there is much controversy as to whether these "jury consultants" are as effective as claimed, but it is a $400 million a year industry with 700 practitioners in 400 firms (Strier & Shestowsky, 1999). One New York trial lawyer emphasized the importance of these consultants when he proclaimed that it was almost an act of malpractice if he did not use a jury consultant when the trial was large or important enough (Strier & Shestowsky).

One poignant example of jury manipulation in hopes of acquittal is the "poison pill" strategy used by a trial consultant named Singer in the Miami River Cops case of 1987. Ms. Singer is reported to have deliberately picked jurors who had personality conflicts with other jurors in hopes they would "explode" and a mistrial be declared. This is a purported popular strategy of jury selection in murder trials whereby the defendant is obviously guilty (Strier & Shestowsky, 1999). If trial consulting is indeed sufficiently effective to affect trial outcomes then this seriously implicates the fairness of jury trials.

Empirical evidence to back the claim of jury consultants is still minimal, but evidence suggests that juror demographic characteristics, personality traits, and general attitudes are associated, albeit weakly, with juror verdicts in mock juries (Moran et al., 1994). Stronger evidence that scientific jury selection can increase the predictability of juror verdicts has been found with real juries. This has been found especially true when the evidence was ambiguous or when specific attitudes toward relevant case matters could be ascertained before trial (Moran et al., 1994). Therefore, these are important considerations in the matter of jury bias and a fair trial for a defendant.

Moran et al., (1994) cited one case whereby potential juror attitudes toward lawyers and drugs were found to be the most important predictors of verdicts in a criminal trial against a lawyer charged with drug crimes. Other studies cited by Moran revealed that attitudes toward Posttraumatic Stress Disorder were determinant in awarding monetary compensation. In addition, attitudes toward battered women were correlated with conviction rates of battered women convicted for murder after killing their batterers (Moran).

The Scientific Jury Selection surveys studied by Moran et al., (1994) indicated that attitudes concerning case relevant variables are better predictors of juror verdicts than are demographic variables. Therefore, it is evident that juror attitudes toward criminals and ethnic defendants may be an important consideration. The literature shows that evidence is not the only decisive factor in deciding guilt or innocence. If potential jurors can be kept off a jury due to language, culture, or religion, then it would appear that jury representiveness of different ethnic minorities would be minimal (Mauro, 2005). How can there be a jury of a defendant's peers when no one on the jury looks or thinks like the defendant?

One finding that appears to be supported in the empirical literature is that the ethnicity of the juror may interact with the ethnicity of the defendant to influence trial outcome. It has been found that the juror is more likely to vote to convict when the defendant is of a different ethnicity than that of the juror (Dane & Wrightsman, 1982; Wuensch et al., 2002). This suggests that ethnic bias may play a role in juror decision-making.

There is a plethora of research that indicates racial bias exists within the criminal justice system especially through bias in juror decision-making due to ethnic differences. Empirical support has been given to the notion that African Americans often receive longer sentences than European Americans, especially when the victim of the crime is European American, the jury is European American, and the defendant is African American (Dane & Wrightsman, 1982).

Mazella and Feingold (1994) conducted 29 experimental studies looking at the relationship ethnicity had on findings of guilt or innocence and recommended length of sentence. This analysis indicated that African Americans received longer sentences than European Americans when the crime was homicide or rape, and European Americans received longer sentences than African Americans did, when the crime was fraud.

Similar findings were made by Gordon (1990) and Gordon et al., (1988), who found that African American burglars received longer sentences than European Americans, but European American embezzlers received longer sentences than African Americans. A consensus from this research was that individuals might receive longer sentences when the crime is stereotypically matched to their ethnicity (e.g., African Americans are viewed as burglars while European Americans are stereotypically viewed as embezzlers) (Wuensch et al., 2002).

Dane and Wrightsman (1982) concluded that jurors are most likely to convict a defendant when the defendant's ethnicity is different from the juror's, rather than when the victim's ethnicity is the same as the juror's. This seems validated by the research of Ugwuegbu (1979) who presented evidence of an interaction between ethnicity of the juror and ethnicity of the defendant when utilizing mock jurors in a simulated trial of a man accused of rape. In this study the ethnicity of the mock jurors were manipulated with one jury being European American and the other being African American. Ugwuegbu found that when the evidence toward the defendant was ambiguous, with no clear findings of guilt or innocence, then jurors tended to find the defendant guilty more often when the defendant was of a different ethnicity than the juror's. Miller and Hewitt (1978) had similar findings with their simulated rape case in regard to victim ethnicity. They found that guilty verdicts were more likely when the victim was the same ethnicity as the juror's, than when the victim was of a different ethnicity.

Abwender and Hough (2001) looked at the interactions between defendant attractiveness and defendant ethnicity, and juror sex and ethnicity. The participants were self-selected and consisted of university students: 89 African Americans (62 female, 27 male), 55 Hispanic Americans (33 female, 22 male), and 69 European Americans (34 female, 29 males). The age range of the sample was 19-51, with a mean age of 24.

Participants were mailed packets that contained the study materials. The packets presented the participants with a case vignette describing a negligent homicide in which alcohol was a factor. There were four vignettes and each varied the physical description of the defendant. The variations were by race (African American or European American) and physical attractiveness (attractive or not attractive). The participants were also given a questionnaire that contained the two dependent variables (guilty or not guilty) rated on a 7-point Likert scale and recommended sentence length in years (0 to 99). In addition, participants were asked to rate their perceptions regarding the attractiveness of the defendant, the likeability of the defendant, the degree of intoxication, and level of responsibility for the incident, also on a 7-point Likert scale.

The directional hypotheses presented were (1) "The attractiveness of the female defendant accused of negligent homicide interacts with participant gender, so that the male participants show a stronger reverse ALE (Attractiveness-leniency effect) than do the female participants" and (2), Defendant race interacts with participant race, so that African American participants show a stronger in-group favorability bias (i.e., greater leniency when the defendant is of the same race) than do European American participants" (Abwender & Hough, 2001, p. 4).

An analysis of variance (ANOVA) was conducted and results found that participants rated the attractive defendant's vignette as more attractive. This rating was not found to be influenced by the defendant's ethnicity or the participant's ethnicity or the participant's sex. A MANOVA was used to analyze the two dependent variables (guilt or innocence), and recommended sentence, with participant sex and defendant attractiveness as independent variables. The only significance found was in relationship to participant sex and defendant attractiveness. The male participants recommended longer sentences for the attractive defendant while the female participants recommended longer sentences for the unattractive defendant. Male participants who rated the defendant as unattractive also tended to rate her as less responsible for the incident.

A two-way MANOVA was conducted on defendant ethnicity in relationship to participant ethnicity, but no overall statistical significance was found except for the African American participants. However, an interaction was found for all participant ethnicities. African Americans gave higher guilt ratings to European American defendants than African American defendants; Hispanic Americans gave higher guilt ratings to African Americans than European Americans; and European Americans rated both African Americans and European Americans similarly. On ratings of sentences, the African American participants recommended longer sentences for European Americans; the Hispanic American participants recommended longer sentences for African Americans, and the European American participants recommended similar sentences for both African American and European American defendants.

This study was interesting in that both African American and Hispanic American participants had more biased responses in regards to the ethnicity of the defendant and determinations of guilt or innocence, as opposed to the European American participants. The authors explained on the basis of previous research that European American participants will "bend over backwards" to appear unprejudiced. If this is so, then European American jury members might make different decisions toward an ethnic minority defendant in order to appear non-racist.

In another experimental study conducted by Wuensch et al., (2002), the researchers manipulated the ethnicity of the litigant (African American or European American) in a simulated case involving a female plaintiff and a male defendant accused of sexual harassment. The researchers did not indicate the ethnic makeup of this final sample, which would be important in understanding the results as it pertains to the general research questions.

The general research question asked in this study was to investigate the interaction of the ethnicity of the defendant, the ethnicity of the plaintiff, and the ethnicity of the juror in a civil law suit. Specifically, the researchers wanted to test the case for European American bias against African American defendants when the victim was European American and the defendant was African American. Research has indicated that African Americans are convicted more often and serve longer terms when the judge and jury members are predominantly European American and the defendants are predominately African American (Wuensch et al., 2002). The specific hypotheses explored were (1) "mock jurors would be more likely to find in favor of the plaintiff, more certain of the guilt of the defendant, and more punitive toward the defendant when the defendant was not of their own race than when the plaintiff was of their own race, and (2), women would be more likely than men to find in favor of the female plaintiff" (p. 2).

The researchers conducted several experiments. They first looked at whether the judgments of European American mock jurors were influenced by the ethnicity of the litigants when a female plaintiff accused her male employer of sexual harassment. The independent variables were sex (male/female), ethnicity of the plaintiff (European American /African American) and the ethnicity of the defendant (European American /African American). The dependent variables were the verdict (innocent/guilty), certainty of guilt rated on a 9-point Likert scale, and the monetary award given to the plaintiff if the defendant was found guilty.

Each participant received a packet with an introduction to the study, instructions, the background of the case, the trial summary, summaries of the litigants' testimony, summaries of the testimony of the litigants' character witnesses, as well as a demographic sheet defining participants by age, sex, ethnicity, and academic standing. The case was presented with a female plaintiff suing for $200,000 in monetary damages. The alleged issue was sexual harassment from her male employer. The participants got a summary of the female plaintiff's side of the issue, which was denied by the defendant's side of the story. The summary of the character-witness testimonies portrayed each litigant in a neutral light, but the ethnicity of the litigant was manipulated, being either African American or European American.

The authors reported they used a logit analysis to evaluate the variables of sex of juror, ethnicity of plaintiff, and ethnicity of defendant on the verdict obtained (guilt/innocence). They found main effects at the .05 alpha level for plaintiff's ethnicity upon the verdict as well as a significant interaction between juror's sex and defendant's ethnicity. Significant results indicate that guilty verdicts were found more frequently (79%) when the plaintiff was European American than African American (59%). When the jurors were male, verdicts of guilty were significantly more frequent when the plaintiff was European American (80%) than African

American (44%) or when the defendant was African American (73%) than European American (50%). Among female jurors the ethnicity of the plaintiff or defendant had no significance.

Wuensch et al., (2002) also used a three-way ANOVA to evaluate the variables of sex of juror, ethnicity of plaintiff, and ethnicity of defendant on certainty of guilt. Significance was found for the interaction of sex of the juror and the ethnicity of defendant, and sex of the juror and ethnicity of the plaintiff. Female jurors were significantly more certain of the defendant's guilt than were male jurors. The researchers did a further analysis on the main effects separately for female and male jurors. The results showed that European American male jurors were significantly more certain of guilt if the defendant was African American rather than European American and was more certain of the defendant's guilt if the plaintiff was European American rather than African American. Findings were consistent for female jurors; as before, ethnicity did not play a significant role in findings of guilt.

Another three-way ANOVA was conducted regarding monetary award. Significance was found for the interaction of sex of juror and ethnicity of the defendant. Findings were that male jurors gave significantly larger awards to the plaintiff when the defendant was African American (M = \$74,407), rather than European American (M = \$26,944). Again, no significance was found with the female jurors.

The second experiment conducted by Wuensch et al., (2002) investigated whether the judgments of African American mock jurors would show the same ethnic bias. The hypotheses stayed the same as in the first experiment. The same sexual harassment scenario was used in this study. The original sample for this study consisted of 172 African American undergraduate psychology students from two public universities also in the Southern part of the U.S. One university was predominately European American and the other predominately African American.

The method, materials, and design of this study were the same as the first. The same logit analysis was used and significance was found for the main effects of sex of juror and ethnicity of the defendant. Female jurors found the defendant guilty significantly more frequently (86%) than did male jurors (70%). As in the first study, guilty verdicts were more frequent when the plaintiff was the same ethnicity as the jurors (84%) for African American plaintiffs vs. European American (71%) although this was not found to be a significant difference in this case.

Male jurors found the defendant guilty significantly more often when the plaintiff was African American (82%) than when European American (58%), but among the female jurors, ethnicity was again not a significant factor. European American defendants were found guilty significantly more often (88%) than were African Americans (67%). Both male and female jurors were significantly more likely to find the defendant guilty if he were European American (Male = 82%, Female = 95%) than African American (Male = 58%, Female = 76%).

A three-way ANOVA was conducted for certainty of guilt and significance was found for the race of the defendant and race of the plaintiff. Certainty of guilt was found to be significantly higher with European American defendants than for African American defendants and significantly higher for African American plaintiffs than with European American plaintiffs.

Another three-way ANOVA was conducted for the amount of money awarded. Significance was found for the race of the defendant. Monetary awards were significantly higher when the defendant was European American (M = $145,193), then when he was African American (M = $90,355). As with the first study, female jurors were found less affected by the ethnicity of the defendant or plaintiff in their juror decision-making and males were found to be more biased. The chances were 11 times greater that a African American male juror would find in favor of a African American female plaintiff when the defendant was European American than when the defendant was African American and the plaintiff was European American. In contrast, for African American female jurors this ratio was only 3.8. These experiments show that the variables of ethnicity of the juror, sex of the juror, ethnicity of the defendant, and ethnicity of the plaintiff need to be further studied.

Bias and Racism

The ethnic makeup of U.S. jails and prisons suggest that there is bias in the criminal justice system. Bias occurs when a person has a prejudiced outlook or unreasoned judgment based on some type of criteria (e.g., race or ethnicity). Bias is often accompanied by racism, which is a belief that race is the primary determinant of human traits, abilities, capacities, and that racial differences determine the superiority of one race over another (Webster, 1993).

Racial prejudice is also defined as the "prejudgment by others that the members of a race are in some way inferior, dangerous or repugnant" to members of groups that typically enjoy power and privilege (Campbell & Marable, 1996, p. 49). Colin and Preciphs (1991) defined racism as "conscious or unconscious, and expressed in actions or attitudes initiated by individuals, groups, or institutions that treat human beings unjustly because of their skin pigmentation" (p. 62).

Models and Theories Pertaining to Ethnic Bias

The social science field has presented numerous bias theories and models in an attempt to explain racism and bias toward ethnic minorities. In a perusal of the literature regarding racism and bias many theories or hypotheses are presented. Many of these theories overlap or complement each other while none seem to be exclusive of all others. Therefore, there is redundancy in ideas. Two models of ethnic bias are discussed, the Culturally Deficient Model and the Scientific Racism Model.

The Culturally Deficient Model. When communities or institutions look upon a part of its membership as culturally deficient because that culture is not a part of the majority European American culture members are marginalized and held as less than worthy. Some ethnicities experience this discrimination more so than others. Similarity to the dominant culture seems to be a mediating factor.

According to Hansman and colleagues (1999), and Oppenheimer (2001), those cultures that are closest in resemblance to Western standards fare the best because they are found less deficient and diverse than those cultures that do not ascribe to Western ideals. In accordance, it is speculated that those ethnicities that came to this country voluntarily to seek opportunity may embrace American ideals more easily. They may assimilate more willingly than those who came involuntarily (e.g., African Americans). Therefore, these ethnicities seem to both "fit in" better and are able to keep psychological distance by not internalizing Western racist notions. In contrast, those ethnicities that came here involuntarily may have a more difficult time not internalizing racist remarks made against them.

Hansman et al., (1999) defined cultural racism as "when power of the majority group plus their racial prejudice results in the exclusions of cultural contributions of historically oppressed groups from textbooks, art, language, and music" (p. 2). Cultural contributions are discounted because they do not meet dominant Western standards. Therefore, these cultural contributions are found deficient. There becomes a culture of power and the rules become a reflection of the culture that has power. Language, especially when used as racial slurs, reinforce that power and continue to minimize and discount based on color and culture (Mahar, 2001; Smith, 1999).

Because the people who represent these discounted ethnic cultures are found deficient it then becomes easier to do terrible things to them because they do not count. It becomes easier to deny them opportunity and even basic freedoms because they are different, they are the "other," and therefore they are inferior and insignificant because they deviate from the dominant culture. Their culture is deemed irrelevant and they are forced to conform to the majority (Hansman et al., 1999; Mahar, 2001; Smith, 1999).

Baratz and Baratz (1969) stated that historically the African American culture has been ignored as an explanation for behavior except for when it held negative connotations. Therefore, the culture of African Americans was seen only as the culture of poverty and positive aspects were not recognized. These authors contended that these ethnocentric concepts have colored psychology's view of this culture and has "forced the interpretation of almost all psychology's data on the Negro into two seemingly dichotomous categories—either that of biological incapacity (genetic inferiority) or social deviance and pathology (environmental deprivation)" (p. 3). Because the U.S. is mythically a "melting pot," cultures that do not assimilate and become westernized are viewed as pathological.

The view of cultural deficiency is often perpetuated through media representations of different cultures. Peretz, editor of *The New Republic* wrote an editorial in 1994 stating specifically that the high out-of-wedlock births seen in the African American community was a direct result of cultural deficiency (Peretz and African American mothers, 1994). When *The Nation* polled editors of other prestigious periodicals such as *The New York Times, The New Yorker,* and *The Washington Monthly* among others, very few found Peretz's remarks racist. Media representation plays a large role in shaping public attitudes and reinforcing racist notions.

Scientific Racism (Genetic Deficient Model). Scientific racism posits that biological inheritance determines the character and behavior of social groups that have been classified into races (Barkan, 1992; Oppenheimer, 2001). Scientific racism promotes the concept that there is a hierarchy of races whereby some are superior (e.g., European American) and most are inferior, and these differences can be ascertained by the sciences (e.g., anthropological, psychological, and medical science) (Jensen, 1967, 1969a, 1969b, 1969c, 1970, 1972;

Oppenheimer, 2001; Rutledge, 1995). Even the word European American denotes racial superiority as Blakey (1999) noted that the word European American has historically referred to racial purity and was thought to represent the original or "uncontaminated" race from which Europeans originated. The European American race is presumed to have come from the Caucus Mountains in the southeastern corner of Europe.

Scientific racism espouses that genetic differences account for variables in certain abilities (e.g., IQ) (Ausdale, 1997; Jensen, 1967, 1969a, 1969b, 1969c, 1970, 1972; Rutledge, 1995). These notions have been used as a foundation to deny certain groups opportunity and bestow privilege onto others (Holloway, 1999). This theory is similar to the culturally deficient model in that some ethnicities are seen as more acceptable than others.

Oppenheimer (2001) stated that within the racial taxonomy some immigrant groups were considered inferior to others depending on how different they were in mannerisms and skin color from Anglo-Saxons. Therefore, the closer one is to looking and acting European American Anglo-Saxon, the more acceptance and social status one can conceivably obtain.

The European American majority has used scientific racism to justify the domination, subjugation, and genocide of other cultures (Barkan, 1992; Oppenheimer, 2001; Rutledge, 1995). For example, slavery was justified because African Americans were not thought to belong to the human race, nor capable of caring for themselves (Garraty, 1996; Pedraza & Rumbaut, 1996).

Scientific racism has also been used for the exclusion of specific ethnic groups from entering the U.S. as was seen in the 20th century when the Johnson act of 1924 excluded Southern and Eastern Europeans from immigrating to the U.S. (Blakey, 1999; Garraty, 1996; Pedraza & Rumbaut, 1996). It has also been used as validation for unethical studies such as the Tuskegee medical experiment in which African American men were denied treatment for syphilis in order to study the advanced effects of this disease (Kohn, 1995). Scientific racism also set the climate for the genocide perpetuated on Native Americans (Oppenheimer, 2001), on Jews during the holocaust, and forms the foundation for apartheid today (Uebel, 1990).

Blakey (1999) stated that in a racist society that believes in European American supremacy the relationship between race and ability often becomes the basis for decisions about the allocation of social resources and the solution to social problems. This can be seen most keenly within the U.S. criminal justice system whereby the majority of those institutionalized are of minority status and/or poor (Allard, 2002; Alvarez & Bachman, 1996; Bureau of Justice Statistics, 2002a, 2002e, 2006; Camp, 1994; Coyle, 2002; Edwards, 2000; Gordon, 1990; Greenfield & Smith, 1999; McDonald & Carlson, 1993; Petersilia, 1983).

In the 1830s, some researchers began the physical measurement of the different races to ascertain abilities (Oppenheimer, 2001). Although craniometry is now obsolete and found to be a false indicator of intellect, the controversy surrounding intellectual superiority of some races over others continues today. In the *Bell Curve* by Herrnstein and Murray (1994), scientific racism is alive and well in their argument that different ethnicities have different intellectual capacities. They claimed the research shows irrefutable proof that Asians have more intellectual capacity than European Americans, and European Americans have more capacity than do African Americans. They stated that the average European American tests higher than 84% of all African Americans and that the average European American scores one standard deviation above that of African Americans.

When there is a belief that biological and genetic differences exist, it becomes easy to look at ethnicities that have been historically denied opportunity as being responsible for their own social position. People from the dominant culture can then point at them and call them inferior and incapable and ignore their own part in the marginalization and subjugation of these minorities. It may also be easier to convict an ethnic minority defendant than a European American defendant due to these beliefs.

Similar attitudes have also been espoused in the eugenics movement. Eugenics seeks to limit the reproductive abilities of those people with low IQs, even so far as to suggest sterilization, while promoting the procreation of people with high IQs to strengthen the race (Taylor, 1981). Many people liken these ideas to Nazism (Barkan, 1992). Although the ideas of eugenics and scientific racism have a long history and go clear back to Galton, these ideas are not obsolete in today's scientific community, and many prominent American and British scientists have supported the eugenics movement (Barkan, 1992; Malik, 1996). For example, as late as 1996 psychologist Christopher Brand's book, *The G Factor*, was denied publication by the publisher John Wiley after Brand declared himself a disciple of Galton and a eugenicist (Malik, 1996).

However, there have also been those who detract from the notion of scientific racism. For example, Boas began challenging conventional ideas about fixed racial types in the 1890s.

Boas and his students, principally Herskovitz, Klineberg, Mead, and Benedict became outspoken regarding their theory, which was the antithesis of scientific racism. Their theory principally stated that culture was primary over biology in explaining human behavior (Barkan, 1992).

Models and Theories Explaining Bias Toward Criminal Defendants

In addition to theories and models that present explanations of ethnic bias, so too are there models and theories that attempt to explain criminality and ethnic bias within the criminal justice system. Minority criminals, or those accused, are doubly discriminated against first for their criminal status and then again for their ethnic status (Mauer, 2001; Mauer & Chesney-Lind, 2003). While many studies have documented bias within the criminal justice system there has not been a definitive answer found to explain the discrepancies between minority and majority individual incarceration rates or length. Several theories have been postulated, but none explains the inherent differences in treatment of persons from minority groups in comparison to the majority ethnic group.

Theories that have been proposed are *conflict theory* (Farnum, 1997; Kaukinen & Colavecchia, 1999; Lilly, Cullen, & Ball, 1989), *social control theory* (Alston, Harley, & Lenhoff, 1995; Down, Robertson, & Harrison, 1997; Giordano, Cernkovich, & Rudolph, 2002; Hirschi, 1969), *labeling theory* (Down et al., 1997; Headley, 2003; Rosenfield, 1997), *general strain theory* (Agnew, 1992; Cloward & Ohlin, 1960; Cohen, 1955; DeFronzo, 1997; Merton, 1938), *societal reaction theory* (Frazier, 1978; Inciardi, 1972), *power threat hypothesis* (Bobo & Hutchings, 1996; Oliver & Mendelberg, 2000; Quillian, 1995), *group position theory* (Green, Srolovitch, & Wong, 1998), and *affect control theory* (Bongkoo & Shafer, 2002; Robinson, Smith-Lovin, & Tsoudis, 1994). However, none of these theories answer the question as to why more minority individuals are incarcerated within the U.S. criminal justice system or why minorities get longer sentence lengths for the same crimes.

Belief in a Just World. The theory most relevant to the current study in explaining juror bias toward ethnic defendants is an individual's belief in a just world. Belief in a just world is thought to be a cultural variable and a part of a person's worldview (Lambert & Raichle, 2000). Therefore, people of different ethnicities should have variations regarding this belief based upon culture. Belief in a just world is seen as an attitude that exists on a continuum between the poles of total acceptance, and total rejection, regarding the notion that the world is a just place (Rubin & Peplau, 1975).

According to the Just World Theory developed by Lerner (1977, 1980) people have a basic need to believe in a just world. An individual who believes the world is just will maintain that certain behaviors deserve certain outcomes. For example, if a person performs bad acts (e.g., robbing banks), then he or she deserves equally bad outcomes (e.g., going to jail), and people who perform good acts (e.g., giving to charity), deserve good things to happen to them (e.g., winning the lottery). Therefore, a person who performs good acts (e.g., giving to charity) does not have bad outcomes happen to him or her (e.g., being arrested) (Lerner, 1977, 1980).

According to Lerner, two primary means are used by individuals to maintain their just world beliefs when evidence presents itself that the world is not a just place. When this happens, an individual might then reinterpret pertinent behavior of self or others or ascribe attributions as to the cause of the unjust event (Lerner & Miller, 1978). Lerner (1980) stated that when a bad thing happens to a good person it upsets the balance. In order to achieve balance the individual will either reassess the event or attribute the outcome as just. The individual might do this by reinterpreting the behavior of the observed person, or by devaluing the observed person, in order to keep a sense of order that the world is a just place.

Culture has been shown to play a role in whether an individual has a high or low belief in a just world. Research has found that people who have a high belief in a just world are generally more religious, authoritarian, oriented toward an internal locus of control, have more admiration for political leaders, hold more negative attitudes toward the disadvantaged, and have more positive attitudes toward existing social institutions (Furnham & Proctor, 1989; Rubin & Peplau, 1975).

Just world belief research has been used to explain individual reactions to the misfortunate and to victims of crime or disease (Furnham & Boston, 1996; Hafer & Olson, 1998; Hillier & Foddy, 1993; Kristiansen, 1990). When a person who believes that the world is a just place sees suffering then he or she experiences dissonance. If the world is just then how could an innocent person suffer?

In order to reduce his or her own dissonance the person who believes the world is just will attribute traits to the person suffering that would explain his or her fate (Hafer & Olson, 1998). The person must be bad or else this bad thing would not have happened. According to this theory, if a person does not do this his or her whole foundation can be shaken and he or she will lose faith in the future. Therefore, to maintain the belief that the world is a just place, in spite of contradictory evidence, the individual will blame the victim (Lerner, 1980; Murray et al., 2005).

The stronger an individual's belief in a just world, the more dissonance he or she will experience when witnessing contrary evidence, and the more he or she will blame the victim for his or her circumstances. Therefore, instead of changing his or her belief from a world that is just, to a world that is unjust, the individual will use cognitive strategies to make the victim's situation fair by attribution (Hafer & Olson, 1998).

Several researchers have looked at Lerner's theory and expanded upon it. Rubin and Peplau (1975) believed that individuals would differ in the amount they would actually believe that the world was just. The general empirical evidence supports that those people who believe in a just world are more apt to believe the person deserved whatever malady or tragedy befell him or her. Therefore, a cancer victim would deserve his or her fate, as he or she must have done something to disserve such a horrible disease.

Bad things do not happen to good people in a just world. People who believe in a just world have also been shown to be more accepting of social injustice or inequities for the same reason (Hafer & Olson, 1998). This logic or thinking can then be extended to defendants accused of a crime. If a defendant were a good person who lived a good life beyond reproach he or she would not be accused of a crime. Theoretically, a juror with high just world beliefs would make attributions about the defendant because if he or she were a good person, he or she would not be accused of a crime.

Just world beliefs can also cause positive psychological attributes and can serve as important adaptive function for an individual (Hunt, 2000). For example, having a high belief in a just world can help individuals psychologically cope with disturbing or catastrophic events (e.g., natural disasters, poverty, racism, rape). Just world beliefs can also help individuals cope with feelings of guilt when comparing themselves to people who are less well off than themselves or when they have survived a disaster and others did not (Carmona, Gorman, Neal, & Bollmer, 1998; Furnham, 1991b). Individuals with high just world beliefs tend to view their world more optimistically and have more life satisfaction (Lipkus, Dalbert, & Siegler, 1996).

Just world beliefs are thought to develop, at least in Western society, through many means such as children's fairy tales, being taught admiration for authority, and through various religious beliefs (Lerner, 1998; Rubin & Peplau, 1975). For example, most fairy tales have a general theme that good deeds are rewarded and bad deeds are punished (e.g., Cinderella is rewarded by marrying the prince, Pinocchio is punished for telling lies by a continuously growing nose, and Santa Claus keeps a list of children who will receive coal because of their "naughty" behaviors during the year).

Rubin and Peplau (1975) discussed that U.S. European American children are taught to (a) respect authority, (b) revere political leaders, and (c) revere American social institutions. However, they also noted that only the virtues of these concepts are usually taught (e.g., a police officer is your friend, Abraham Lincoln walked miles to return a penny, and George Washington could not tell a lie). Rubin and Peplau theorized that fairy tales and stories about political leaders carry with them the idea that power and prestige are symbols of value. They hypothesize that children who are brought up in such a manner will be more likely to believe in a just world.

Religions such as Judaism and Christianity also teach just world values. Many religions ascribe to the idea that people are rewarded in heaven for their good deeds and sinless lives. In contrast, those less worthy because of bad deeds or a sinful life will be punished in hell. Furthermore, the Protestant work ethnic espouses that the virtues of hard work will be one day rewarded with financial success (Rubin & Peplau, 1975). As children grow into adults, their beliefs that the world is just and "people deserve what they get," are reinforced or disputed by their personal experiences. For example, those individuals who have been discriminated against because of racism, have been victims of crime, or have experienced other unjustness, probably would eventually refute the idea that the world is a just place.

Belief in a just world has been extensively researched with regard to *victims of rape or assault* (Furnham & Boston, 1996; Hillier & Foddy, 1993; Kristiansen, 1990), *marital abuse* (Lipkus & Bissonnette, 1996), *personal misfortune* (Hafer & Olson, 1998), *hostility in abuse victims* (Nelson, 1992), *irrational beliefs* (Durm & Stowers, 1998), *religiosity* (Begue, 2002; Crozier & Joseph, 1997), *personal responsibility* (Braman & Lambert, 2001), *unjust societies* (Ferguson, 2000; Glennon, Joseph, & Hunter, 1993; Joseph & Stringer, 1998), *perceptions of discrimination* (Lipkus & Siegler, 1993), *occupation* (Mohr & Luscri, 1995), *mood, and attitudes toward victims* (Kershaw, 1997), *right-wing authoritarianism* (Lambert. 1999; Lambert, Burroughs, & Nguyen,1999), *moral norms* (Kaiser, 2003), *emotional response* (Hafer & Correy, 1999), *unjust world beliefs* (Dalbert, 2001), *health and coping style* (Furnham, 1995), *self-esteem* (Glennon, 1993), *attitudes toward homosexuals and/or AIDS* (Furnham, 1992; Glennon, 1993), *working women* (Hafer, 1993), *psychological well-being* (Lipkus et al., 1996), and *between cultures* (Furnham, 1991a).

Several studies have looked at jury bias and just world beliefs. Lambert and Raichle (2000) found that verdicts of guilt and sentencing length were often determined by individual judgments of personal blame and that despite having the exact same evidence perceivers come to different conclusions based upon personal variables held by individual jury members. Lambert and Raichle also stated that most social psychology textbooks assert that just world beliefs play a causal role in blaming a victim for his or her own misfortune.

Even so, O'Quin and Vogler (1989) pointed out that very little attention has been given to punishment reactions or reactions toward defendants of crime. This has remained true in the ensuing years and has been an area overlooked in the research literature. Of those studies that have looked at defendants of crime several have found support that just world beliefs play a role in defendant sentencing.

For example, Finamore and Carlson (1987) found that high beliefs in a just world are related to crime control attitudes. They found high just world beliefs related to an assumption that the defendant was guilty and the belief that the police make few mistakes, and therefore, no sympathy should be wasted on those accused of a crime. Lerner (1980) found that jurors with high just world beliefs have been more likely to give harsher sentences to defendants accused of heinous crimes such as negligent homicide.

Just world beliefs are further implicated as a factor in juror decision-making by the research conducted by Rubin and Peplau (1975). Their research suggests that when the defendant directly caused a victim's suffering then the juror with high just world beliefs would seek to restore justice for the victim. Therefore, in an attempt to restore justice and salvage their own just world beliefs a juror may show punitive attitudes toward the defendant and demand vengeance. Consequently, it seems surprising that so little research has been conducted using mock jurors to ascertain what relationship just world beliefs have compared to defendant sentencing. How jurors perceive a defendant's guilt is important. Are jurors with high just world beliefs basing their decisions upon what is presented as evidence in the trial or are they trying to salvage their faith that the world is just by their actions?

Lambert and Raichle (2000) conducted two exploratory studies looking at the role of political ideology in mediating judgments in the blame toward rape victims and defendants. Specifically, these authors wanted to explain why politically conservative individuals would assign more blame to the victim of a rape than participants who held more liberal political views. These authors looked at the hypotheses of just world beliefs, personal responsibility, and legitimization, as an attempt to explain this phenomenon. However, even though they stated they had strong a priori predictions as to whether any of the individual difference variables would be stronger for males than for females, they chose not to state them for this research.

The three independent variables considered for the first study was level of conservatism, just world beliefs, and the sex of the participant. Just world belief was operationalized by using the Just World Belief (JWB) scale by Dalbert and Lipkus (as cited in Shaw & Wright, 1967). Conservatism was operationalized by a self-report measure of conservatism and another for liberalism (Lambert & Raichle, 2000). The dependent variable was the amount of blame assigned to both the victim and the defendant of the crime in a vignette given to the participants.

The authors used a sample of 57 undergraduate psychology students (27 men and 30 women) who received $6.00, or class credit, for participation. Unfortunately, the authors did not specify demographic variables such as the ethnicity, socioeconomic status, or specific age range for this sample. In addition, this small, convenient sample makes it difficult to generalize the results of this study to any population outside of the particular institution where the study was conducted.

The procedure of this study was to gather students for a “mass-testing” of personality dimensions prior to the main study. Students were asked to rate how conservative or liberal they were on two Likert scales, one for each construct, ranging from 0 -10. As can be expected, these two scales were found to be somewhat negatively correlated (r = -.55), if a participant scored high on conservatism, they scored low on liberalism. It does not appear that the liberalism scale was needed, as it did not add new information. No reliability or validity coefficients were reported for these self-measures.

Participants were also given the JWB scale at this time and were asked to express agreement or disagreement of statements based on a Likert scale ranging from (1 = strongly disagree) to (6 = strongly agree). This version of the JWB scale was reported to have a high level of internal reliability ($r = .81$). This scale was also found to be somewhat correlated with the conservatism index scale ($r = .19$). However, there were no significant differences between men and women concerning JWB scores. It is unfortunate that these researchers did not state directional hypotheses so that definitive statements could be made.

Two months after participants completed the above assessments they were gathered again under the assumption they were participating in a completely different study. They were given instructions that the purpose of the current research was to study how people react to information about the past history regarding the dating and sexual history of two individuals within a given scenario. Participants were told the case vignette they were to read was not sexually explicit. However, participants were given a choice to participate in this study, or complete a different study, that did not look at dating and sexual history.

The second part of this first study looked at individual differences in social dominance orientation (SDO). This instrument measures the degree that participants are motivated to maintain or eliminate hierarchical relationships between dominant and nondominant groups (e.g. men and women). For this study the researchers did state directional hypotheses, which were (a) the SDO will be positively correlated with blaming the female, but negatively correlated with blaming the male, (b) the SDO will be positively correlated with certain types of conservative beliefs/attitudes and negatively correlated with liberal beliefs/attitudes, and (c) the SDO scale would predict blaming judgments to a greater extent that would the Protestant Work Ethic scale (PWE). The Protestant Work Ethic scale was used to measure conservatism and is believed to be associated with the degree to which participants hold others as personally responsible for their actions or outcomes (Lambert & Raichle, 2000).

The design of this study, as stated, could induce several internal threats such as history or mortality due to the two-month interval between the initial assessments and this phase of the study. The authors do not state if all the participants returned to participate in the next stage of this study. None of the statistical analyses reported degrees of freedom so the reader has no way of knowing how much attrition occurred.

For the second phase of this study, participants were given a vignette depicting a date rape between a female victim and a male defendant. After reading the vignette, students were given a series of questions to answer designed to measure their perceptions of the victim and the defendant. The format was that half of the participants were asked to judge the victim first and the defendant second; the other half had the reverse order. Questions for both the victim and defendant addressed participant perceptions regarding how much blame should be assigned to the victim, or to the defendant, for what had happened. Participants were asked to rate their perceptions on a Likert scale of, (0 = not at all to blame) to (10 = much to blame). Participants were also asked to rate the likeability of both the victim and the defendant with respect to the traits of aggressiveness, confidence, immaturity, intelligence, stubbornness, and honesty (Lambert & Raichle, 2000).

Results showed that participants blamed the male assailant over that of the female victim. However, an in-group favoritism was also found regarding sex of the participant and level of blame toward the defendant or victim. Female participants blamed the male defendant more than did the male participants, whereas male participants blamed the female victim more than the female participants (Lambert & Raichle, 2000). The hypothesis that just world beliefs would impact perceptions of blame was not supported in this study. In fact, just world beliefs in this study were found to have no impact on whether participants judged the female victim or the male defendant.

With regard to conservatism, Lambert and Raichle (2000) found conservatism to be positively correlated with blaming the female victim and also with judgments of blame toward the male defendant. Participants who scored high on conservatism were found to blame the female victim more and the male defendant less. Even though these results were found to be significant the correlations were moderate at best.

This research is important because it looks at the defendant of a crime instead of just the victim. However, this study only looked at assignment of blame rather than guilt or innocence, or sentence length. The study also used the assignment of blame in a manner that participants had to decide who held more blame, victim or defendant, rather than look at just the defendant and their beliefs about his guilt or what would be a just sentence.

In the second study conducted by Lambert and Raichle (2000), an attempt was made to delineate the role conservatism played on victim blaming. The same vignette was used, and the independent variables remained conservatism, just world beliefs, and participant sex, as in the first study. However, conservatism was operationalized differently than in the first study. Scales used were the Social Dominance Orientation scale developed by Sidanius, Pratto, and Bobo (as cited in Lambert & Raichle), and the Protestant Work Ethic scale developed by Katz and Hass, (as cited in Lambert & Raichle). The same a priori hypotheses were used as noted above.

The Social Dominance Orientation scale and the Protestant Work Ethic scale were used because they were thought to measure the construct of conservatism and test the legitimization hypothesis more effectively than the previous self-report measures. The legitimization hypothesis postulates that conservative individuals would be more likely to legitimize existing hierarchical relations between dominant groups (males) and non-dominant groups (females). According to this hypothesis, a social dominance orientation would be positively correlated with blaming the female victim and negatively correlated with blaming the male defendant. It would also be expected that a social dominance orientation would be positively correlated with conservatism and negatively correlated with liberalism.

Participants for the second study included 139 undergraduate psychology students (47 men, 92 women) who received class credit for participation. Again, Lambert and Raichle (2000) do not give pertinent demographics that would be useful for the present study such as ethnicity or socioeconomic status. While this sample is larger than that obtained in the first study little information is given to ascertain external validity.

The procedure for the second study was to administer the Social Dominance Orientation scale, the Protestant Work Ethic scale, the same Just World Beliefs scale used in the first study developed by Dalbert and Lipkus, as well as the Just World Beliefs scale developed by Rubin and Peplau (Lambert & Raichle, 2000). In addition, participants were asked to rate their attitudes toward conservatives and liberals on a Likert scale with a range of (-5 = strongly dislike) to (+ 5 = strongly like).

Results of the second Lambert and Raichle (2000) study duplicated the findings of the first in that participants assigned more blame to the male defendant overall and the same sex effect was found. However, in this second study a sex effect was only found for the female victim. Male participants blamed the female victim more than did the female participants.

Findings were also that scores on the Social Dominance Scale were negatively correlated with judgments of the male defendant and positively correlated with judgments of the female victim. The higher participants scored on the Social Dominance Scale the less they blamed the male defendant and the more they blamed the female victim for the date rape. It was also found that individuals who endorsed liking liberalism tended to blame the male defendant and tended to not blame the female victim.

The Rubin and Peplau Just World Belief Scale was successful in delineating between participants blaming the victim or blaming the defendant. Participants with high scores on this scale tended to blame the female victim more often than the male defendant. This was only true for this scale and not the Dalbert and Lipkus scale. However, neither of the just world belief scales significantly predicted judgments toward the male defendant in this study.

Regression analyses showed significance that scores on the Social Dominance scale were negatively correlated with blaming the male defendant and liberal attitudes were positively correlated with blaming the male defendant. Sex was not found to moderate either of these variables. Scores on the Social Dominance scale and attributions of blame were similar. Attitudes toward liberalism and blame were also similar between males and females.

Findings were similar when looking at blame attributed to the female victim. Scores on the Social Dominance scale were positively correlated with attributions of blame of the female victim and liberal attitudes were negatively correlated with blame of the female victim. Again, there was no sex differences found for the Social Dominance scale or liberal attitudes.

The implication of the Lambert and Raichle (2000) study is that factors other than the evidence presented influenced participant attitudes of blame attributed, to either the victim, or the defendant of a date rape. This is an important implication in the study of juror bias with regard to explaining the racial disparity within the criminal justice system. Just world beliefs were not found to be a strong predictor in the attribution of blame in the first study, and only moderately so in the second; these beliefs have not been tested in attributions of guilt or recommendation of sentence length. Blame for an event cannot be considered the same as guilt for an act. Using a crime vignette that holds emotional value such as date rape could have skewed results for this study. It would be important to look at a crime that holds no emotional value.

In addition, no attempt was made by Lambert and Raichle to control for participants who have had negative experiences in dating, have been victims or defendants of rape, or date rape, or have had a friend or family member who was a victim or defendant, which is a potential threat to the internal validity of these two studies. In addition, no demographic data were used to identify the ethnic identity of the participants, nor was the ethnic identity of the victim or defendant stated. Since a belief in a just world has been noted in the literature to be a cultural variable (Lerner, 1980), ethnic differences on this scale would be important to measure.

Another study by O'Quin and Vogler (1989) looked at the relationship just world beliefs had to participant perceptions toward the defendant and victim of crime in relationship to just and unjust sentencing outcomes for the defendant and location of the robbery. Participants included 52 inmates (no sex specified) taking college level courses in a maximum-security prison and 106 introductory sociology students from a public 4-year university (35 males, 71 females). This sample may be just as difficult to generalize to the general U.S. population as the study conducted by Lambert and Raichle (2000). This is due to the mixed nature of the sample such as inmates vs. university students, as well as differences in age, socioeconomic status, ethnicity, sex, and also because the university students only came from one introductory sociology course.

Once again, there were no demographic data available to ascertain the ethnicity of the participants, which is a variable that should be considered. In addition, both groups of students received credit in their classes for participating in this study. This may have created a participation bias. Theoretically, only students needing credit may have participated in this study and they would be different from those who did not need credit. As is often the case this was a sample of convenience.

One glaring omission O'Quin and Vogler made with regard to this sample is that they did not state whether the public university students had ever been convicted of a crime, the victim of a crime, arrested, robbed, or had ever worked for the criminal justice system. These variables might influence the outcome of this study when comparing an inmate group with a non-inmate group. These researchers noted in their literature review a study conducted by Sarat (as cited by O'Quin & Vogler, 1989) who found that persons having firsthand knowledge or experience with the criminal justice system tend to be more dissatisfied with this system then those who have had no contact with it. Furnham and Proctor (1989) stated that the single most important factor in whether or not an individual believes in a just world is his or her own experiences with injustice.

Participants filled out the Just World Belief scale by Rubin and Peplau (1975), read a vignette, which described a robbery between a male victim and a male assailant, and then answered questions concerning their perceptions of the victim, defendant, and defendant's sentence. These assessments were filled out within the participant's regular classroom and were given by the class instructors of each institution. Therefore, the environment and the principle person conducting the research were different for the two groups of participants and could have had an impact on the ensuing results.

The independent variables in this study were the Just World Belief scores, the location in which the crime was committed, and the sentence length of the defendant. The dependent variable was a questionnaire consisting of 11 questions regarding participant perceptions of the victim and the defendant. These researchers used a case vignette of a robbery in which the sentence for the defendant varied. Half the participants received a vignette where the sentence was short (6 months with 1 year of parole) and the other half a vignette in which the sentence was long (5 to 15 years in prison). The researchers believed that the short sentence represented a more "just" punishment, whereas the long sentence represented an "unjust" punishment.

The researchers also varied the location in which the crime was committed. In half the vignettes the crime was committed in a good part of town and in the other half the bad part of town. The researchers hypothesized this would have an impact on victim blaming. Theoretically, it would be harder to blame a victim who was robbed in the good part of town as opposed to the bad part of town.

One research hypothesis explored in the O'Quin and Vogler (1989) study was that inmates would have lower scores on the Just World Belief scale than would non-inmates. O'Quin and Vogler also hypothesized that inmates would be more sensitive to the defendant sentencing manipulation and the public university student participants would be more sensitive to the crime location manipulation. It makes sense that those incarcerated may have differing opinions regarding responsibility for a crime, blame for the victim, and hold different attitudes toward sentencing, than those who presumably have never been incarcerated. Another hypothesis was that participants with high Just World Belief scores would blame the victim regardless of the circumstances presented whereas those with low scores would only blame the victim when it was easy to do so (e.g., he or she was robbed in the bad part of town). The final hypothesis presented was that high JWB scorers would be more likely to perceive the defendant's sentence as just.

Upon completion of the JWB scale and the perception questions the researchers split the participants into two groups (inmate students and public students) at the median based upon their Just World Belief scale scores (high or low). No significant difference was found in the just world beliefs of inmate student participants versus that of the public student participants.

However, as the researchers did not ascertain whether the public student group had any prior history with the criminal justice system, it is difficult to reach conclusions regarding how alike or unalike these two groups may be outside of the fact that one group was currently incarcerated. It could be that several participants within the public student group may have had prior contact with the criminal justice system either as defendants or as victims. This may have made their scores on the JWB scale similar to that of the inmate group.

O'Quin and Vogler (1989) further analyzed the public student group of participants to determine if there were any sex differences as this was the only mixed sexed group. The authors used a *t*-test with the JWB scores to determine if there was a difference in scores based upon sex of the participant. No significance was found. A MANOVA was then used with the 11 perception questions as the dependent variables in a 2 (sex of participant) x 2 (sentence: just, short sentence vs. unjust, long sentence) x 2 (Victim: easy to blame, bad part of town vs. difficult to blame, good part of town) x 2 (JWB high scores vs. low scores). No significance was found.

However, significance was found for Just World Belief scores with a univariate analyses for three of the dependent variable questions concerning participant perceptions toward the defendant. The a priori hypothesis was that high JWB scorers would perceive the defendant's sentence as just. It was found that participants with high JWB scores:

- Were more likely to believe the defendant's sentence was just.
- Were less likely to state they liked the defendant.
- Were less likely to express sympathy for the defendant.

Concerning the manipulation of the crime scene (bad part of town vs. good part of town) significance was found for four of the questions pertaining to participant perception of the victim. The a priori hypothesis was that high JWB scorers would blame the victim regardless of the circumstances whereas low JWB scorers would only blame the victim when it was easy to do so (e.g., victim was in the bad part of town). Overall, when the crime occurred in the bad part of town, participants reported they:

- Liked the victim less.
- Had less sympathy for the victim.
- Thought the crime was more the victim's fault.
- Were more likely to blame the victim instead of the defendant.

However, even though these results are interesting, O'Quin and Vogler (1989) do not report whether these participants had high or low JWB scores, which is what the hypothesis directly stated. The hypothesis stated was that participants with high Just World Belief scores would blame the victim regardless of the circumstances presented whereas those with low scores would only blame the victim when it was easy to do so (e.g., he or she was robbed in the bad part of town). Therefore, while significance was found, it does not relate directly to the hypothesis stated or at least it is difficult to determine because the JWB scores were not reported.

The effect of sentencing justness was found to be significant for six of the dependent variable perception questions. The a priori hypothesis stated was that high JWB scorers would be more likely to perceive the perpetrator's sentence as just. It was found that when the defendant received a long sentence participants were more likely to report the perception that:

- The sentence was less just
- The defendant did not deserve the long sentence
- The defendant was less responsible for the crime
- Felt more sympathy for the defendant
- Felt the crime was more the victim's fault
- Reported they liked the victim less

Once again O'Quin and Vogler (1989) do not report the JWB scores that would confirm their hypothesis. Therefore, it is difficult to ascertain the relevance of this data, as it is not reported in the manner consistent with the hypothesis. However, the study conducted by

O'Quin and Vogler is important because it looked not only at perceptions toward victims, but also at perceptions toward the defendant. This study found significance for the relationship of just world beliefs to perceptions toward both the victim and the defendant in a crime. However, O'Quin and Vogler only studied the participant perceptions with sentencing already established and only looked at perceptions of blame. It would be interesting and beneficial to further the research on jury bias to have participants step into the role of juror and have to make decisions on sentence length.

Rubin and Peplau (1975) reported two studies that have not been published that held interesting results. An unpublished pilot study by Izzett (as cited in Rubin & Peplau) looked at participant reactions to a criminal defendant based upon scores of the JWB scale. The participants acted as mock jurors in a negligent homicide case. It was found that participants with high JWB scores formed a significantly less favorable opinion of the defendant than did participants with low JWB scores and tended to assign stiffer sentences.

Gerbasi and Zuckerman (as cited in Rubin & Peplau, 1975) researched participants with real jury experience in a mock trial. They found that jurors with high JWB scores gave more severe verdicts than did participants with low JWB scores. Why these studies have not been published in not known. However, both indicate further research in just world beliefs as it pertains to jury bias is warranted.

It is a fact that ethnic minorities are arrested more often, convicted more frequently, and have served longer sentences than European Americans even when the crimes committed are exactly the same (Alvarez & Bachman, 1996; Bureau of Justice Statistics, 2002a, 2002b, 2002c, 2002e, 2006). Therefore, the evidence presented at trial does not seem to play as crucial a role in declarations of guilt or innocence, or sentencing, as U.S. citizens and the criminal justice system would like to believe. It is critical then to look at juror beliefs and attributions of guilt. Many theories have been postulated, but one that has been mostly overlooked in the literature is the juror's belief in a just world.

The few studies conducted that have looked at just world beliefs in relationship to defendants indicate that this is a phenomenon worth pursuing in research. Yet, this is not the direction just world belief researchers seem to be headed. While multiple studies have shown just world beliefs to be a powerful factor in the perceptions, attitudes, and social behavior of individuals, very few have addressed a juror's just world beliefs in relationship to their perceptions toward a criminal defendant (Lambert & Raichle, 2000; O'Quin & Vogler, 1989) and only a handful of studies have looked at just world beliefs in relationship to jury bias toward a criminal defendant. This is an important oversight in the literature. If just world beliefs have been found to be an important factor in the attribution of victim blame would it not then be an important factor in attribution of guilt toward an ethnic minority defendant?

Multicultural Factors Affecting Bias Toward Minority Defendants

Of the many factors that could influence juror bias culture and ethnicity play a large role. Cultural variables are prolific and several are discussed such as ethnicity, religiosity, sex, cultural socialization, worldview, locus of control, and cultural beliefs about crime and punishment.

Ethnicity

Ethnic minorities are disproportionately affected by the criminal justice system. Therefore, odds are increased for a member of one of these populations to have either been incarcerated or else have a close friend or family member who has been incarcerated (Bureau of Justice Statistics, 2002a, 2002b, 2002c, 2002e, 2006). Hypothetically, ethnic minorities might have more empathy towards criminal defendants and therefore hold attitudes that are more lenient toward them.

On the other hand, individuals of the European American dominant culture are less represented within the criminal justice system and might see criminal defendants as belonging to ethnic groups other than European American. In addition, in trying to maintain European American dominance in the increasing ethnic stratification of America (Doane, 1997), European Americans might hold a more egocentric self-image of their cultural group and hold negative stereotypes about other groups (Brinson & Morris, 2001; Hurwitz & Peffley, 1997; King, 1993; Sokefeld, 1999). As the majority of defendants incarcerated are of ethnicities other than European American, European Americans might hold more punitive attitudes toward criminal defendants.

Religiosity

Different cultures often practice different religions and this too may play a role in attitudes towards defendants and crime. For example, Leiber and Woodrick (1997) reported that Christian fundamentalism was found to be a strong predictor of support for the use of corporal punishment, the death penalty, and attitudes toward punitiveness in general. In addition religious beliefs, specifically a literal elucidation of the Bible, were correlated positively with ethnic and sex stereotyping and with punitiveness toward criminal defendants or those incarcerated.

Sex and Gender

Sex and gender can also play a role in how one perceives defendants and crime. Boys and girls are socialized to play different roles within society. Girls are stereotypically thought to be more nurturing, expressive, and perhaps forgiving. In contrast, boys are thought to be more aggressive, instrumental, and harsh (Berndt, 1997). Therefore, it could be hypothesized based upon stereotypical gender socialization that females would have more lenient attitudes toward criminal defendants than would males. An experimental study conducted by Wuensch and colleagues (2002) supported this notion.

Many studies have also shown there are differences in perception and interest between sexes in many areas. One study showed there were differences in interest in political affairs between the sexes and that differences in gender socialization across racial and ethnic groups could aggravate sex differences in political orientation (Alozie, Simon, & Merrill, 2003). Another indicated that, at least for wife battering, there was a significant difference between the sexes as to whether an individual reported the crime to police (Mwamwenda, 1999). Another study showed there were sex differences in attitudes toward many issues, such as labor unions, jobs, and employers (Schur & Kruse, 1992). Therefore, it is probable that males and females might hold different beliefs or attitudes toward inmates, crime, and punishment.

In addition, the combination of sex and ethnicity can also shape attitudes. For example, a Hispanic American female may hold different views than a Hispanic American male due to gender role socialization. It has been hypothesized that the racial variations in employment and family patterns may cause ethnic minorities to hold more traditional gender-related attitudes than do European Americans (Eisenman & Dantzker, 2006; McGoldrick, Giordano, &

Pearch, 1996). However, contradictory studies of sex-related attitudes show that attitudes vary across ethnic groups depending upon the type of attitudes addressed (Kane, 2000). A study conducted by Nielsen (2000) found that experiences with, and legal attitudes toward, offensive public speech varied by ethnicity, sex, and social class.

Cultural Socialization

Lifelong effects of racism might also cause differences in attitudes. Many ethnicities deal with racism and discrimination on a daily basis, which might profoundly affect their perceptions toward others. Members from the dominant culture generally do not face such racism, but instead are benefited from "White privilege," a phenomenon discussed in many multicultural publications whereby European Americans are afforded privileges within the dominant European American society that other ethnic groups do not enjoy (Ancis & Szymanski, 2001; McIntosh, 1989).

Worldview

Different cultures also hold different worldviews. Worldview can be thought of as the lens through which individual's see their world. Different cultures wear different lenses. Worldview represents the beliefs, values, and assumptions an individual or society holds about the world, people, nature, time, and relationships.

There are many aspects of worldview such as collectivism vs. individualism, locus of control/locus of responsibility, time orientation, human activity, social relations, and people/nature relationships. Those aspects of worldview that are most germane to this study and are seen to be most impactful toward cultural bias toward criminal defendants are collectivism vs. individualism and locus of control/locus of responsibility. These are discussed below in relationship to how culture may impact a juror's perception of a criminal defendant.

Collectivism vs. Individualism. Cultural groups differ on the dimension regarding group cohesion, some are collectivist, and some are individualist. Collectivist societies work together for the advancement and welfare of the group and value cooperation. Individualist societies value independence, competition, and place individual success over that of group success (Sue & Sue, 1999). European American culture represents an individualistic society whereas Hispanic American, African American, and Native American cultures represent collectivist societies.

With regard to crime and criminal defendants, people in collectivist societies might view a defendant from their group as having let down the community and be more biased toward that individual. In contrast, people in individualistic societies might view these defendants as entities separate from the community and would take no personal offense or interest in the criminal defendant's alleged crimes.

Locus of Control/Locus of Responsibility. Some cultures have an internal locus of control and some an external locus. An internal locus of control places responsibility on the individual for his or her actions, whereas an external locus of control removes blame from the individual and places it on external factors such as poverty, lack of education, or low socioeconomic status (Sue & Sue, 1999). Therefore, societies with an internal locus of control might blame the individual, while those with an external locus of control might blame societal forces. Conceivably, this might affect attitudes and biases toward those that break the law (Na & Loftus, 1998) and in fact research on the Rubin & Peplau Just World Belief scale indicates it correlates significantly and predictably with locus of control (Furnham & Proctor, 1989; Maes, 1998a).

Acculturation

Ethnic individuals who have acculturated to the U.S. dominant European American culture may have beliefs more similar to European American culture than to the culture of their ethnic heritage. Redfield, Linton, and Herskovits (1936) stated that acculturation is comprehensive of "those phenomena which result when groups of individuals sharing different cultures come into continuous first-hand contact, with subsequent changes in the original culture patterns of either, or both groups" (p. 149).

Through the acculturation process, ethnic individuals may modify both their behaviors and values. Behavioral change might include changing the dominant language spoken or the level of participation in both their own, and the new group's, cultural events. Value change might include the preferred interpersonal relational style, ideas about the person-nature relationship, beliefs about human nature, and orientation to time (Kim & Abreu, 2001). In this manner, acculturation can have a moderating impact on ethnic differences between participants or jurors.

Cultural Beliefs toward Crime and Punishment

People in different cultures are socialized differently and therefore might hold different behavioral scripts, schemas, or attitudes. Diverse cultures and societies deal with criminals and crime differently. Some countries are very punitive, and some have policies of public whipping, disfigurement for criminal offenses, and/or capital punishment. Other countries are more lenient and focus efforts on rehabilitative efforts and social supports rather than punishment (Na & Loftus, 1998). Therefore, culture may play a role in how crime is viewed and punished.

Ethnic differences relating to an individual ethnic group's experiences within the criminal justice system may also lead to different perceptions regarding this system and an ethnic person's role within it. A study conducted by Wortley (1996) explored the relationship between racial differences in the perception of criminal justice in Toronto, Canada. This study is interesting because the Canadian government and judicial system incorporates an official policy of multiculturalism and does not purport to have the racial conflict that occurs within the U.S. (Wortley).

The 1994 general population survey was used to obtain a random sample representative of the population of African Americans, European Americans, and Chinese, 18 years or older living in Toronto. Potential participant households were called by phone using random digit dialing and the adult member with the most recent birthday was the selected participant for that household. Because of this sampling procedure external validity and generalizability should be high. The response rate for the survey was 60%. The resulting sample size was 1257, including 417 African American, 405 Chinese, and 435 European American respondents.

Demographic data suggests that the sample contained proportionately an older group of European Americans, (25% were over the age of 55), in comparison to African Americans (11%) and Chinese (13%). This might result in cohort effects, meaning that those in the age group of 55+ might have significant historical, sociological, or political events that have shaped them as a group and formed values or beliefs in relationship to their collective history that would not be present for those under the age of 55 in the same way. The sample also included a smaller proportion of African Americans who were educated and a higher proportion that were unemployed. Therefore, the extraneous variables of age, education, and employment might confound this study.

The purpose of the survey was to (a) document the perception of racism within the Ontario criminal justice system, (b) determine if these perceptions vary by race or other demographic variables, and (c) investigate whether observed differences in perception can be explained by actual experiences with police and the court system. Results of the survey indicated that more African Americans (75%) felt there was discrimination toward African Americans within the criminal justice system than either European Americans (50%) or Chinese (50%). The participants were asked if they thought people were treated fairly in the criminal justice system. Specifically they were asked:

1. Are poor people treated the same as rich people?
2. Are young people treated the same as old people?
3. Are men treated the same as women?
4. Are English speaking people treated the same as non-English speaking people?
5. Are African American people treated the same as European American people?
6. Are Chinese people treated the same as European American people?

These questions were asked on two levels:

1. In relationship to police.
2. In relationship to judges.

A bivariate analysis was used to examine the racial differences in perception of differential treatment by the criminal justice system. The analysis found that people felt the police discriminate more often than judges. African American respondents (75%) believed there was more discrimination over all, then either European American respondents (50%), or Chinese respondents (50%). More European American respondents felt there was discrimination based upon age, social class, and sex, then either African Americans or Chinese. African American respondents (38%) felt African Americans were treated worse than European Americans than European American respondents (16%) or Chinese respondents (12%). African American respondents (55%) felt that the police were more likely to use force against African Americans, then did Chinese (42%) and European American (33%)

respondents. African American respondents (48%), more so than European Americans (29%) and Chinese (29%) respondents, felt that African American defendants would get longer sentences than European Americans for the same crime. The results suggest that ethnicity has an influence on the perceptions of fairness within the criminal justice system.

The authors pointed out that race alone does not account for the disparity in perceptions. They pointed out that the African American respondents were younger and came from lower socioeconomic backgrounds than either the European American or Chinese respondents. Therefore, the authors used a regression analysis to test for the variables of race, age, sex, education, income, employment status, marital status, and place of birth, to determine if there were any statistically significant predictors of perceived injustice. The results indicated that the differences in perception of criminal injustice could not be totally explained by demographic factors. Even after controlling for age, sex, education, income, employment status, marital status, and place of birth, race was still significantly related to perceptions of discrimination.

In addition, all respondents were asked about prior experience under the criminal justice system from routine "pull overs" (being stopped by the police) to having to appear in criminal court, and these variables were controlled in the study. Respondents were asked if they were stopped by the police while (a) driving a car, (b) walking on the street, (c) walking in a shopping mall or other public place in the previous two years. These responses were coded as an ordinal variable. Respondents who had not been stopped were coded '0,' those who had been stopped once were coded '1,' and those who had been stopped two or more times were coded '2.' Respondents were asked if they, a family member, or a friend, had ever appeared in an Ontario criminal court as a person accused of a crime. This variable was coded 1 = court contact, and 0 = no court contact.

The researchers examined the answers to these questions. More African Americans (43%) had experienced being stopped by police within the previous two years as compared to European Americans (25%) and Chinese (19%). African Americans (34%) also reported being stopped by police on two or more occasions in comparison to European American (17%) and Chinese (14%).

The study is relevant to the present research because it makes an illustrated point that demographic factors alone cannot account for perceptions of bias within the criminal justice system. Even within a system that ascribes to multiculturalism participants felt that discrimination existed. The U.S. criminal justice system has no such multicultural policy. This study demonstrates the need to look beyond demographic factors as a predictor of juror bias or perceptions of discrimination.

A different study by Jackson and Ammen (1996) looked at the attitudes of correctional officers towards inmates and whether or not the ethnicity of the officer made a difference in their attitudes toward inmates. They noted that the composition of corrections officers was changing from the traditional European American male to a mix that contained more ethnic minorities and women. The researcher's purpose for the study was to see if this change in composition had any impact on officer/inmate relations. The question they researched was, Are Hispanic American and African American correctional officers, as compared to European American officers, more or less punitive in their attitudes toward treatment programs for inmates?

Jackson and Ammen selected a systematic random sample from all uniformed correctional officers employed in the Texas Department of Criminal Justice. They used the main computer terminal of the Texas Department of Criminal Justice-Institutional Division (TDCJ-ID) to locate the names of all employees. They then selected every 10th name on the roster. The sample reflected the actual population in that it contained 21% female, 79% male, 22% African American, 10% Hispanic American, 5% Asian, 5% Native American and 67% European American. The mean age was 36.0 years. This is comparable to the actual population of Texas Corrections officers so this study would be generalizable to Texas Corrections officers, but perhaps not to corrections officers in other states.

All the selected participants were mailed a survey consisting of 76 items. All surveys were coded to ensure confidentiality. The response rate for the first mailing was 34%. A second mailing was conducted, which brought the total number of participants to 476, increasing the response rate to 48% overall. In order to ensure a large enough sample of minority officers participants were also obtained from those attending a yearly in-service training. Participation from this group was 100% for an additional 377. The total participant number for this study then was 853.

Using the in-service training officers might have generated different responses than the random sample. The in-service training officers had someone interview them versus the random sample that had surveys mailed to them. It is possible that within the second group of in-service officers there could be an interview bias impact from being interviewed versus having a confidential survey to fill out. The second group of officers might have been concerned with how they responded. They may have been concerned with a social bias or may have felt pressure from their peers or supervisors to answer in a specific manner. There are also problems with selection as the second group of officers was selected because they were already a part of a pre-established group.

The authors conducted a *t*-test for differences in the proportion of the two groups and found that there was not a significant difference between the in-service group and the random sample group on response rate. Therefore, the authors concluded that the high consistency among the items indicated a lack of bias between the two participant sets. They also concluded their total sample was representative of the larger population.

The dependent variable was the nature and orientation of the correctional officers' attitudes toward the selected treatment programs for inmates. In other words, do the officers support rehabilitation efforts that go beyond the basic custodial requirements as measured by their attitudes toward these programs? The survey consisted of two instruments to measure the dependent variables, an attitude scale toward specific prison programs, and a punitive orientation scale by Klofas and Toch (1982).

The first instrument consisted of 59 dichotomous items with total possible instrument scores ranging from 0-59. This scale was further divided into six subscales each representing a possible attitude toward a specific program (the academic educational program through the secondary level, the medical program beyond basic and preventative health care, the psychological counseling program, the college program, religious programs and vocational programs that included welding, woodwork, and plumbing).

Cronbach's alpha reliability coefficients for internal consistency for these six subscales were adequate to good, ranging from .66 to .76. The scale in its entirety had a Cronbach's alpha coefficient of .92. This seems to be a good reliable measure, however no validity information was included so it is difficult to ascertain that the scale measures what it purports to measure.

The measures of punitiveness for this study came from the Klofas and Toch (1982) instrument and was a four-factor measure of: *counseling roles* (e.g., (a) rehabilitation programs should be left to mental health professionals, (b) counseling is a job for counselors, not officers, (c) if an officer wants to do counseling, he or she should change jobs), *social distance* (e.g., an officer should work hard to earn trust from inmates), *concern with the corruption of authority* (e.g., you can never completely trust an inmate), *and punitive orientation* (e.g., there would be much less crime if prisons were more uncomfortable). There were no statistics regarding the reliability or validity of this measure.

A multiple regression was used to ascertain whether the ethnicity of an officer played a role in his or her attitudes towards inmates and levels of punitiveness versus leniency. The results indicated a lack of statistical significance that ethnicity had an impact. The authors also used an analysis of variance. However, having unequal cell sizes they used Scheffe's post hoc test with an alpha level of .05. Another problem the authors encountered was that minority officers of any number was a new addition in the Texas penal system at the time of this study, therefore, they thought seniority or age of the corrections officer might also play a role on attitudes toward inmates. It was hypothesized that European American officers would hold more seniority and be older than the minority officers. Hypothetically, these two variables might have a relationship to attitudes.

Therefore, one-way ANOVAs were used to test for significance of these two variables on the three groups of European Americans, Hispanic Americans, and African Americans. No significant results were found on seniority, but an effect was found relating to age. It was found that the European American officers were older (M = 34.5) than both the Hispanic American officers (M = 31.1), and African American officers (M = 33.5) and that there was a slight correlation between age of the officer and support for programs.

The authors reported that African American officers had more support for rehabilitation programs than European American officers did over all and that African American officers were supportive of extended vocational, academic (through high school), college, religious, and medical services for inmates than the European American officers. They also reported that Hispanic American scores were similar to the European American scores but the smaller sample size (n = 80) may have interfered with findings of significance for this group. These researchers also noted that both the Hispanic American officers and the European American officers were less supportive of extended medical services for inmates than the African American officers and that there were no significant differences in attitudes towards the three groups in terms of psychological services. Overall, they found that European American and Hispanic American officers trusted inmates less, felt that the prison environment should be more harsh and punitive, and were less likely to feel that counseling or helping the inmate was a part of their job, then did the African American officers.

Another aspect of cultural differences toward crime and punishment are studies that show racial attitudes play a role in support of the death penalty. Studies by Aguirre and Baker (1991) and Bohm (1991) have found that people who support the death penalty also support racist attitudes. Finckenauer (1988) has observed that public support for the death penalty is linked to personality characteristics such as racial prejudice. Taylor, Scheppele, and Stinchcombe (1979) and Stinchcombe et al., (1980) have shown a strong positive correlation between European American attitudes of opposition toward busing ethnic minorities into European American neighborhood schools for racial equality and European American support for capital punishment. Research supports that ethnic minorities are also disproportionately found on death row and subjected to the death penalty then are European Americans (D'Alemberte, 1992; Hurwitz & Peffley, 1997; Study Shows, 2000). There is also evidence that the ethnicity of the victim influences sentences of death and that the chance of a death sentence for those that kill European Americans is 4.3 times greater than for those that kill African Americans (Radelet, 1995).

It is evident that racism and bias against minorities exists within the criminal justice system, and it is evident that ethnicity of the defendant, and ethnicity of the juror might play a role in the formation of this bias. There have been many postulated theories of bias, including: *the social pathology model* (Baratz & Baratz, 1969), *scientific racism* (Barkan, 1992; Herrnstein & Murray, 1994; Seligman, 1992), *societal reaction theory* (Bernstein, Kelly, & Doyle, 1977; Blakey, 1999; Ericson, 1977; Fraizer, 1978; Inciardi, 1972), *group position theory* (Blumer, 1958; Bobo & Hutchings, 1996), *cultural deprivation theory* (Clark, 1972), *control theory* (Down, Robertson, & Harrison, 1977), *labeling theory* (Down et al.), and *social threat hypothesis* (Liska & Yu, 1992).

In addition, many cultural variables might lead one juror to hold certain beliefs that another juror of a different culture may not. All of these variables theoretically should have an impact on juror decision-making. One variable that has not been explored in relationship to jury bias toward a criminal defendant is a juror's just world beliefs. Whether one believes in a just world, and that one deserves that which one gets, may have an important impact on juror decision-making and bias toward a criminal defendant in the courtroom.

Instruments

There are always multiple ways of measuring any construct. The following section briefly discusses the instruments currently available to measure the constructs of belief in a just world and attitudes toward criminal defendants.

Belief in a Just World Measures

There have been several scales developed to measure just world beliefs. These scales have been used with various amounts of success in different populations and variables. One factor hindering research on this scale is that nearly every just world belief researcher has come up with his or her own derivative of the original Rubin and Peplau (1975) scale. Following is a discussion on the merits and drawbacks of the main scales used most often.

Rubin and Peplau (1975), the Just World Belief Scale. This is a 20-item scale with 10 questions endorsing that the world is unjust, and 10 questions endorsing that the world is a just place from the domains of traffic, law, education, sports, history, and health (Maes, 1998a). Questions typical for an unjust persuasion include, "It is a common occurrence for a guilty person to get off free in American courts," or "Careful drivers are just as likely to get hurt in traffic accidents as careless ones." Questions representative of a just world orientation include, "Men who keep in shape have little chance of suffering a heart attack," or "It is rare for an innocent man to be wrongly sent to jail" Rubin and Peplau (1975) believed that this scale taps an underlying belief in a just world on a single continuum.

The Rubin and Peplau (1975) scale has been primarily used with university students in the U.S. and Canada (Hafer & Correy, 1999; Rubin & Peplau, 1975) but has also been used in other countries (Furnham & Proctor, 1989), with inmates (O'Quin & Vogler, 1989), and with participants with ages ranging from 17 to 60+ (Braman & Lambert, 2001; Furnham & Boston, 1996). Primary ethnicities used have been Chinese, European American, and African American (Furnham & Boston).

The Rubin and Peplau Scale has an internal consistency between .38 (prison inmates) and .83 (university students) (Braman, & Lambert, 2001; Maes, 1998a; Rubin & Peplau, 1975).

Predictive validity was established through the Rubin and Peplau 1971 study (as cited in Rubin & Peplau, 1975). Construct validity has also been demonstrated for this scale in several unpublished studies cited by Rubin and Peplau (1975). Numerous studies have been conducted to validate this scale and it has been generally found to be valid.

Dalbert and Lipkus Just World Belief Scale (as cited in Lambert & Raichle, 2000). This is an 18-item instrument that has been used successfully in a variety of studies conducted by Lambert and Raichle. Participants using this scale are asked to respond to a series of statements indicating their agreement or disagreement on a Likert scale ranging from (6 = strongly agree) to (1 = strongly disagree). Questions representative of this scale are "In general, I think that there is justice in the world" and "Overall, events in my life are just." The internal consistency reported by Lambert and Raichle is (r = .81). No validity estimates were given. Lambert and Raichle used this scale with a sample of university students in the field of psychology. A literature review found no other current research that has used this version of this scale.

The Global Belief In A Just World Scale (as cited in Furnham, 1998). This is a 7-item instrument scored on a 6-point Likert scale ranging from agree to disagree. This scale has been used primarily with university students with an age range of 16 to 18 (Crozier & Joseph, 1997). Reliability coefficients have been reported from .79 to .82 and concurrent validity has been reported (Furnham).

The Multidimensional Belief in a Just World Scale (Furnham, 1998, 2003)**.** This is a 30-item scale with an 8-point Likert scale of strongly disagree to strong agree. However, it does not ascribe to a one-dimensional view of just world beliefs. It yields six different scores for scales that measure several different aspects of just world beliefs, such as (Crozier & Joseph, 1997; Durm & Stowers, 1998; Furnham & Boston, 1996; Furnham & Proctor, 1989):

- Personal just world beliefs (control over the nonsocial environment such as in personal achievement).
- Interpersonal just world beliefs (control over other people individually or in groups).
- Societal just world beliefs (control over social, economic, and political events).

Questions typical of this scale include "When I get lucky breaks it is usually because I have earned them," "Outward-going, sociable people deserve a happy life," and "It is rare for an innocent man to be wrongly sent to jail." Many of the questions for this scale have been taken from the Rubin and Peplau scale.

The Furnham and Proctor scale (1998, 2003) has been used with university psychology students in the U.S., Australia, Britain, Germany, Greece, Hong Kong, India, Israel, New Zealand, West Indies, Zimbabwe, and with White South African school children (Furnham, 1991b). The age range of participants administered this scale is 16 to 18 (Crozier & Joseph, 1997). Reliability coefficients range from .58 to .63 and construct validity has been found, but no details were given (Furnham, 1998).

Attitudes Toward Criminal Defendants Measures

Few scales focus on perceptions toward criminal defendants or punishment for their crimes. The few that have been found through an extensive literature review are highlighted.

Attitudes Toward The Punishment of Criminals Scale (Wang & Thurstone, 1931 as cited in Shaw & Wright, 1967). This is a 34-item scale to be used with college students and is said to have been constructed using University of Chicago students. A version has also been created to use with high school students. This is a weighted questionnaire and not a Likert scale. The questions are primarily concerned with the participants' perceptions as to how, or if, criminals should be punished.

Questions typical of the Attitudes Toward the Punishment of Criminals scale include "Hard prison life will keep men from committing crime," and "It is wrong for society to make any of its members suffer." This first question noted has a weight of 9.0, the second a weight of 1.1. High scores indicate the participant has a favorable attitude toward the punishment of criminals. In other words, the participant is in favor of harsh punishment for convicted defendants. This participant would more likely recommend longer sentences than would those participants scoring lower on this scale.

Reliability coefficients range from .57 to .76 (Ferguson, 1944a, 1944b; Lorge, 1939) and test-retest reliability .66 (Thurstone, 1932). Content validity has been found by correlating this scale with Thurstone's Attitude Toward Capital Punishment scale with coefficients ranging from .30 - .50 (Diggory, 1953).

Attitudes Towards Prisoners Scale (Melvin, Gramling, & Gardner, 1985). This is a 36-item 5-point Likert scale with responses of disagree strongly, disagree, undecided, agree, and agree strongly. Each item receives a score between 1 and 5 where (1 representing the most negative attitude) and (5 representing the most positive attitude) toward prisoners. A high positive total score indicates that the participant views prisoners as normal people capable of positive change while a negative total score indicates the participant views prisoners as essentially deviant and incapable of positive change.

Questions typical for the Attitudes Toward Prisoners scale are as follows: "Most prisoners are victims of circumstances and deserved to be helped," or "Give a prisoner an inch and he will take a mile." The reliability scores for this scale as reported in Melvin et al., (1985) are as follows: split-half reliability .84-.92 using five different samples. Test-retest reliability was .82. No validity coefficients were reported.

Deterrence Scale (Cullen, Cullen, & Wozniak, 1988). This is 5-item 7-point Likert scale ranging from (1) very strongly agree to (7) very strongly disagree. This scale measures attitudes regarding participant beliefs that longer sentencing will deter crime. Questions typical of this scale include "Stiffer jail sentences will help reduce the amount of crime by showing that crime does not pay" or "Sending criminals to jail will not stop them from committing crimes." Cronbach's alpha coefficient established reliability at .80. No validity coefficients were reported in the literature.

***Punitive Orientation* Scale** (Klofas & Toch, 1982). This is a 4-item 4-point Likert scale that measures the degree to which a participant supports a punitive orientation toward the treatment of inmates within the prison or jail environment and whether services should be provided. Questions typical of this scale include "Rehabilitation programs are a waste of money" or "There would be much less crime if prisons were uncomfortable." This scale ranges from (1 = Strongly agree) to (4 = Strongly disagree). Many studies have used this scale and the Cronbach's alpha coefficient has been reported from .63 (Whitehead & Lindquist, 1992) to .72 (Farkas, 1999) to .91 (Simourd, 1997). No validity coefficients were cited in the literature.

Rehabilitation Orientation Scale (Cullen, Lutze, Link, & Wolfe, 1989). This is a 9-item 7-point Likert scale that measures support for rehabilitation. The scale ranges from (1) very strongly agree to (7) very strongly disagree. Several studies have tested reliability of this measure and results range from .58 (Burton, Ju, Dunaway, & Wolfe, 1991) to .83 (Robinson, Porporino, & Simourd, 1993). No validity coefficients were reported. Questions typical of this scale are, "All rehabilitation programs have done is to allow criminals who deserve to be punished to get off easily" or "Rehabilitating a criminal is just as important as making a criminal pay for his or her crime."

Implications of the Literature

The issue of juror bias and racial disparity within the criminal justice system is an important topic that needs further exploration because as the director of the Neighborhood Defender Service of Harlem said,

"We cannot run society for the privileged and allow a significant proportion of the population to be marginalized. It impacts the quality of life for all of us if we have "throw away" people. A justice system which tolerates injustice is doomed to collapse" (Reducing Racial Disparity, 2000, p. 3).

Researchers do not have access to the jury deliberation room or process. Consequently, there have been primarily two methods for studying juror decision-making: Archival analyses and mock jury experiments (MacCoun, 1989). In the archival analyses approach, researchers take a sample of jury verdicts from the court record and look at statistically evident trends or relationships between verdicts and case characteristics. However, these findings are after the fact and often omit a great deal of data that was not available to the researcher (MacCoun).

With the mock juror approach, researchers are able to engage in controlled experiments with random assignment to test variables of interest. In this way, researchers can isolate variables and test them statistically to ascertain the impact or relationship that a particular variable, or cluster of variables, have on jury decision-making. Since real juries cannot be manipulated or studied except ex post facto mock jury studies are the best solution for researchers wishing to explain juror bias. As the current study is interested in the relationships between a juror's just world beliefs, his or her ethnicity, his or her attitudes toward the punishment of criminals, and the defendant's ethnicity to juror bias, the latter method was used.

An analysis by Lambert and Raichle (2000) found that when looking at the role just world beliefs play in victim blaming, two types of research designs have primarily been used. The first approach has been the random assignment of participants to conditions in which just world beliefs are likely, or are not likely, to contribute to blame of the victim. There is no measure of individual differences in just world beliefs that accompany this approach.

The other approach has generally measured individual differences in just world beliefs and then used these differences to predict participants' judgments and behavior. The first method has been used more frequently than has the second, and has found more empirical support (Lambert & Raichle, 2000). However, neither of these approaches has been used with a mock juror in determination of sentence length for criminal defendants.

In an attempt to predict juror behavior, the second approach appears more salient. The purpose of the current research was to understand juror bias. By looking at individual differences in a juror's Just World Beliefs and in scores on the Attitudes Toward the Punishment of Criminals scale, predictions can be made in regard to juror decision-making toward criminal defendants. For the purposes of this study, juror decisions were recorded on a juror decision record.

The current study looks at the relationship of a juror's just world beliefs, his or her ethnicity, and the ethnicity of the defendant to juror bias as measured by the Attitudes Toward the Punishment of Criminals scale. It is hypothesized that just world beliefs can impact punitive attitudes toward criminal defendants in a jury trial, because in order to keep the belief that the world is "just," a jury member must attribute what has happened to the defendant as being what he or she "deserves." In other words, an innocent person would not be accused of a crime, and therefore, the defendant must be guilty. It is further hypothesized that individual jury members who hold a punitive attitude toward the punishment of criminals recommend more punitive (longer) sentences.

While some research indicates a minority juror would be harsher in judgment on a defendant of his or her own ethnicity (King, 1993; Miller & Hewitt, 1978) other research implies that a minority juror who is the same ethnicity as the defendant would be more lenient in the sentencing of that defendant. This is thought to be due to the psychological need to maintain a positive self-image (Broeder, 1959; Crocker et al., 1994; Dane & Wrightsman, 1982; Enomoto, 1999; Johnson et al., 2002; King, 1993; Montada, 1998; Murray et al., 1997; Sellers et al., 1998; Smith, 1991; Valk & Karu, 2001; Verkuyten, 2003; Wuensch et al., 2002; Yueh-Ting & Ottati, 2002).

It seems logical that individuals of ethnic minority groups would have lower just world beliefs then those individuals of the majority European American group due to ethnic experiences of racism. When one finds continual prejudice that hinders his or her ability to achieve success in areas of socioeconomic status, educational opportunity, and/or employment, and whose ethnic group is severely over-represented in the criminal justice system, it seems reasonable that he or she would probably not believe that the world is just.

It also seems reasonable that Hispanic Americans would hold less punitive attitudes toward criminals than European Americans based upon the racial disparity within the criminal justice system. Statistics show that African Americans and Hispanic Americans are over-represented within the U.S. criminal justice system as compared to European Americans. Therefore, the likelihood is greater that Hispanic American participants would have had more contact with this system either individually or through family and friends. This would be expected to shape attitudes toward the punishment of criminals in the direction of having attitudes that are more lenient and less biased toward a criminal defendant.

It would seem reasonable that juror bias is complexly caused and many factors contribute to its existence. Many factors may therefore interact to explain why ethnic bias occurs within the U.S. criminal justice system. Juror bias research indicates that a juror tends to convict a defendant of his or her own ethnicity less often than the same juror convicts members of other ethnicities (Dane & Wrightsman, 1982; King, 1993; Wuensch et al., 2002).

Summary

Social scientists have extensively studied the antecedents of racism, jury bias, and the ethnic discrepancy inherent in the criminal justice system. Each piece of research illuminates another piece of the complexity behind these phenomena. Many theories have been postulated with regard to each of these constructs.

One promising theory that has had borne fruitful results in explaining research participants' perceptions of victims is the Just World Belief theory postulated by Lerner (1977, 1980). A plethora of research as described before has looked at personality traits and individual differences in how people perceive the fate a victim receives whether it is for rape, robbery, or a disease. However, only a handful of research studies have looked at a participant's just world beliefs in regard to a criminal defendant convicted of a crime.

It seems if significance has been found that just world beliefs would affect a participant's or juror's perception toward the victim of a crime, and have an impact on monetary amounts awarded, then certainly it should have an impact on perceptions toward a criminal defendant and determination of sentence length. None of the just world belief research has looked at juror attitudes toward a criminal defendant, juror attitudes toward the punishment of criminals, nor the possibility of a relationship between these attitudes, the ethnicity of the participant, and the ethnicity of the defendant.

CHAPTER THREE
Methods

This chapter discusses how participants were selected, the sampling procedure, the instruments used, when and how data was collected. This chapter also discusses how missing data was handled, the list of independent and dependent variables under study, and provides the research hypotheses presented in relation to those variables. In addition, the statistical analysis is described, as well as, the assumptions and delimitations of the current study.

Participants

Participation in this study was limited to Hispanic American and European American volunteers as these were the two main ethnicities represented on the campus from which participants were recruited and were also two of the main three ethnicities (African American, Hispanic American, and European American) represented in the literature regarding juror bias and bias within the criminal justice system. African American participants were not recruited due to the low numbers of African American students at the campus where this study took place.

The total number of original participants for this study was (N = 116). Because this research was interested in examining possible ethnic differences in juror bias between Hispanic American and European American mock jurors data from those participants who identified as a primary ethnicity other than Hispanic American or European American (n = 11) were not used. Further, since this study identified participants as all those individuals who completed all aspects of the study, some participants were not used due to incomplete data (n = 15). Therefore, the remaining participant pool used in this study was (N = 90).

Participant demographics were 91% female (n = 82) and 9% male (n = 8), 44% European American (n = 40), 56% Hispanic American (n = 50). Participant age ranged from 17-52, with a mean age of 24. Data was also collected regarding the socioeconomic status of participants using Hollingshead's Two Factor Index of Social Position (Miller, 1983). Four participants did not provide enough information to ascertain their SES so their data was not included in the total. Therefore the following results included only 86 participants instead of 90.

The results of this analysis showed that 7% ($n = 6$) of participants had an SES factor of class I, which is the highest SES category. Category one represents the wealthiest fifth of the nation; 47% ($n = 40$) had a SES factor of class II, 24% ($n = 21$) had a SES factor of class III, 15% ($n = 13$) had an SES factor of class IV, and finally 7% ($n = 6$) had a SES factor of class V, the lowest category and represents the poorest fifth of the nation. The majority of participants fell into classes II and III, indicating a moderately high SES status among the majority of participants.

Sampling Procedure

Participants were recruited from undergraduate and graduate classes from a large southwestern university. Participants were solicited through classes such as "Viewing the Wider World." This is a program that requires students in a college (e.g., College of Education) to take two classes outside of their college in order to receive their degree. This ensured a greater mix of majors represented in the study than just counseling and psychology majors.

Participants were recruited for this study through faculty who taught classes under the Viewing the Wider World, heading. These faculty were identified and sent an e-mail explaining this study and were also asked to consider giving students extra credit for their participation in this study. The explanatory e-mail had an attachment for a flyer they could print out and pass among their students.

The flyer contained a World Wide Web link to this study, which was conducted online through www.psychdata.com. In addition, flyers with this link were posted in various places around campus and on the "thank you for participating" page that participants received when completing the study. On the thank you page, there was an explanatory clause that stated participants could e-mail the study link to fellow students they thought might be interested in participating in this study if they were so interested. PsychData was founded in 2001 and is a professionally developed and maintained web site, which utilizes state-of-the art technology combing a centralized database with strict security policies and procedures that simplifies data collection for researchers.

Instrumentation

Constructs often have multiple methods to measure them. Researchers continuously try to find better scales that have higher validity and reliability than previous scales. Sometimes this can create confusion for researchers as to what scale should be used and the literature review to find satisfactory scales becomes daunting. In the end, the researcher must choose a scale that has the highest reliability and validity of all other options. However, the researcher must also choose the best scale that measures the concept in the same way the researcher conceptualizes it or else the researcher much change his or her conceptualization. For these reasons, the best scales for this research study were the Just World Beliefs scale by Rubin and Peplau (1975), and the Attitudes Toward the Punishment of Criminals Scale (Wang & Thurstone, 1931 as cited in Shaw & Wright, 1967).

Just World Belief Scale (Rubin & Peplau, 1975). This is a 20-item scale with 10 questions endorsing that the world is unjust and 10 questions endorsing that the world is a just place from the domains of traffic, law, education, sports, history, and health (Maes, 1998a). Questions typical for an unjust persuasion include, "It is a common occurrence for a guilty person to get off free in American courts," or "Careful drivers are just as likely to get hurt in traffic accidents as careless ones." Questions representative of a just world orientation include, "Men who keep in shape have little chance of suffering a heart attack," or "It is rare for an innocent man to be wrongly sent to jail" It is believed that this scale taps an underlying belief in a just world on a single continuum (Rubin & Peplau).

A Likert scale is used for participants to indicate their level of agreement to the scale questions with a range of 1 (strongly disagree) to 6 (strongly agree). The scale uses a total score with a range from 1 (represents a total rejection of just world beliefs) to 6 (represents a total acceptance of just world beliefs). The total score is derived by adding together the individual question Likert items, and then dividing that total by 20 to get the mean score. In the sample used by Rubin and Peplau (1975) with 90 male and 90 female Boston University students, the mean score was 3.08.

The Rubin and Peplau Scale has been primarily used with university students in the U.S. and Canada (Hafer & Correy, 1999; Rubin & Peplau, 1975) but has also been used in other countries (Furnham & Proctor, 1989), with inmates (O'Quin & Vogler, 1989), and with participants with ages ranging from 17 to 60+ (Braman & Lambert, 2001; Furnham & Boston,

1996). Primary ethnicities used have been Chinese, European American, and African American (Furnham & Boston).

This scale typically scores between r = .38 (prison inmates) and r = .83 (university students) on internal consistency tests (Braman & Lambert, 2001; Maes, 1998a; Rubin & Peplau, 1975). The Cronbach's Alpha for the sample in the current study was r = .62. Predictive validity was established through the Rubin and Peplau 1971 study (as cited in Rubin & Peplau, 1975) whereby participants were randomly assigned "good or bad lottery numbers" in the 1971 national draft lottery for the Vietnam War. Participants filled out the Just World Belief scale, drew their lottery numbers, and then listened to a radio broadcast indicating those participants to be drafted. Participants were then asked to rate their fellow participants on a variety of dimensions.

Most participants expressed greater sympathy, greater liking, and less resentment for those participants who lost the lottery and were drafted. However, those participants who scored high on the JWB scale had the opposite feelings. Those with high JWB scores resented the losers more than the winners and had about as much liking for both winners and losers (Rubin & Peplau, 1975). These perceptions were consistent regardless of the participant's own fate in the lottery.

Construct validity has also been demonstrated for the Just World Belief scale in several unpublished studies cited by Rubin and Peplau (1975). Zuckerman et al., (as cited by Rubin & Peplau) conducted an unpublished study in which participants watched a fellow student presumably receive electric shocks as part of a supposed learning experiment. Those participants with high JWB scores derogated the victim significantly more than did participants with low JWB scores. High JWB scorers also felt the research was more important and less cruel. In another unpublished study by Zuckerman et al., (as cited by Rubin & Peplau) participants were presented with a vignette depicting a rape. It was found that participants who scored high on the JWB scale blamed the victim more than did lower scorers.

Research on the Just World Belief scale indicate it correlates significantly and predictably with other measures for the following constructs: Trust, religiousness, protestant work ethic, authoritarianism, conservatism, locus of control, adaptability, political attitudes, social attitudes, personality, and voting preferences (Furnham & Proctor, 1989; Maes, 1998a). Numerous studies have been conducted to validate this scale and it has been generally found to be valid. This scale has been used for over 25 years by researchers investigating the construct of just world beliefs, and in fact, over half of the JWB studies published in English have used this scale (Furnham, 1998, 2003; Furnham & Proctor, 1989).

Many factor analyses have been done on the Just World Belief scale. One factor analysis conducted by Fink and Wilkens (as cited by Maes, 1998a), determined that this scale is not one-dimensional, but instead, yielded three different factors: (1) Deserving (e.g., you get what you give), (2) denial of injustice, and (3) judgment of a just world. The first factor is reported to explain 65% of the variance (Maes). Other factor analyses have been conducted but no uniform results have emerged (Furnham, 2003).

In summary, the Rubin and Peplau Scale has been used extensively with the population from which a sample is desired for the current research, which is university students. In the few studies conducted that looked at participant perception of a defendant, this scale successfully delineated between high scores and low scores. Therefore, this scale was used for this current study.

Attitudes Toward The Punishment of Criminals Scale (Wang & Thurstone, 1931, as cited in Shaw & Wright, 1967). This is a 34-item scale designed to be used with college students and was developed with University of Chicago students. A version has also been created to use with high school students. This is a weighted questionnaire and not a Likert scale. The questions are primarily concerned with the participants' perceptions as to how, or if, criminals should be punished. The scale has possible scores ranging from 0 to 186.2 due to the weighted scores. A person could achieve a score of zero if the person did not endorse any of the items on the scale and could achieve a score of 186.2 if a person endorsed all items on the scale. Low scores indicate lenient attitudes toward the punishment of criminals while high scores indicate punitive attitudes toward the punishment of criminals.

Questions typical of the Attitudes Toward the Punishment of Criminals scale include "Hard prison life will keep men from committing crime," and "It is wrong for society to make any of its members suffer." This first question noted has a weight of 9.0, the second a weight of 1.1. The participant's score is configured using the scale values of the items for which he or she agrees. High scores indicate the participant has a favorable attitude toward the punishment of criminals. In other words, the participant is in favor of harsh punishment for convicted defendants. This participant would more likely recommend longer sentences, than would those participants scoring lower on this scale.

Reliability coefficients range from (r = .57) to (r = .76) (Ferguson, 1944a, 1944b; Lorge, 1939) and test-retest reliability (r = .66) (Thurstone, 1932). Content validity has been found by correlating this scale with Thurstone's Attitude Toward Capital Punishment scale with coefficients ranging from (r = .30) to (r = .50) (Diggory, 1953). The Cronbach's alpha for the sample in the current study was (r = .70). While this scale's psychometric properties are only adequate, this scale measures more effectively what the current study is trying to measure: Influences of juror bias (punitiveness) toward criminal defendants.

Juror Decision Record. This was a form created by the researcher, which asked participant mock jurors to choose a sentence they felt fair and just for the criminal defendant described in the case vignette. The participants were given a choice for sentencing, which contained an array of options. These choices ranged from zero months in prison (probation) to 36 months in prison. These choices followed the sentencing guidelines for the crime depicted in the case vignette for the state in which this study was conducted.

Data Collection

Data were collected from undergraduate and graduate students from the general population who volunteered to participate in this study. Participants were given a web link to www.psychdata.com to participate in this study. When participants used the link they were taken directly to the informed consent page (see Appendix A). If participants clicked on the "I accept" button at the bottom of the informed consent page they were acknowledging consent for the study and were then able to begin their participation of the study. If participants clicked on the "I do not accept" button they were taken to a "thank you for your participation" page. Participants who completed the study were also taken to the "thank you for your participation" page at the end of their participation. This page could then be printed as proof of participation and turned in to professors who gave extra credit points for participation in a study. No other incentives were used for recruitment for this study. Data was collected from March 1, 2005 to March 31, 2005.

Demographic sheet. When participants entered the study they were given a demographic sheet (see Appendix B) to fill out, which asked them to identify their sex (e.g., male or female), their age, and the ethnicity with which they most identified (e.g., Hispanic American or European American). It was explained they had to choose one or the other and to choose the one that best fit for them. Those participants that were bi-ethnic were asked to choose the ethnicity for which they most identified culturally. Information regarding socioeconomic status (SES) was also gathered using the Hollignshead Two-Factor Index of Social Position (Miller, 1983). No personal identifiers were collected (e.g., name, social security number).

Case Vignette. After filling out the demographic sheet, the participants were given a defendant case vignette in which the ethnicity of the criminal defendant was randomly assigned by computer. A participant could have received a criminal defendant who was European American, Hispanic American, or African American (see appendices C, D, and E). After reading the case vignette, participants were asked to fill out the Juror Decision Record (see Appendix F), the Just World Beliefs Scale (see Appendix G) and the Attitudes Toward the Punishment of Criminals Scale (See Appendix H). Due to the nature of www.psychdata.com at the time of this study, measures could not be counter-balanced so the above order was used. The intent was to have the participant make his or her decisions about the case and record those on the juror decision record prior to filling out the scales so that their decisions were not influenced by the scales.

The case vignette consisted of a defendant biography and arrest card, the arresting officer's report, the investigating officer's report, the victim statement (see Appendices C, D, & E), and the juror decision record form (see Appendix F). The case vignette was designed to present a case as closely as possible to a real life case and presented the participants with information they would have in a real trial situation. The case vignette was the same in all detail for all participants except for the ethnicity of the defendant, which was manipulated. The vignette depicted a 25-year-old male construction worker who was convicted of felony burglary. The evidence for conviction was based on circumstantial evidence that the defendant drove by an open garage that contained a number of tools. Witnesses described the defendants truck parked near the open garage at the time of the theft. The range of time for participants to read the case materials and complete the assessment packet was 30-45 minutes.

Missing Data. Participants were operationally defined as those volunteers who complete all aspects of the study. If a volunteer did not complete all portions of the study, he or she was not considered a participant. After data was downloaded from www.psychdata.com each participant's data was checked for completeness. Those that were not completed were not included in the analysis.

Variable List

The independent variables for this study were ethnicity of the juror, ethnicity of the defendant, and Just World Beliefs scale scores. The Just World Belief scale was an independent variable for hypothesis number four only. These variables were coded in the following way:

- Ethnicity of the juror (1 if European American, 0 if otherwise) and (1 if Hispanic American, 0 if otherwise).
- Ethnicity of the defendant (1 if African American, 0 if otherwise), (1 if European American, 0 if otherwise), and (1 if Hispanic American, 0 if otherwise).
- Just World Beliefs Scale is a continuous variable (hypothesis four). Scores range from 1 (total rejection of just world beliefs) to 6 (total acceptance of just world beliefs). Each juror had a score on this scale.

The dependent variables for this study were the juror decision record, Attitudes Toward the Punishment of Criminals Scale, and the Just World Beliefs Scale. The Just World Belief scale was used as a dependent variable on hypothesis number one.

- Juror Decision Record: Individual juror decisions for sentencing (0 months to 36 months) with the choice of zero indicating the juror chose probation only for the criminal defendant. This was a continuous variable and all participants had a score within the range of 0-36.
- Attitude Toward the Punishment of Criminals scale: It is a continuous variable with a score range of 0 to 186.2 due to the weighted scores. A person could achieve a score of zero if the person did not endorse any of the items on the scale and could achieve a score of 186.2 if a person endorsed all items on the scale. Low scores indicate lenient attitudes toward the punishment of criminals while high scores

indicate punitive attitudes toward the punishment of criminals. Each juror had a score on this scale.

- Just World Beliefs Scale: It is a continuous variable scores range from 0 – 6. Each juror had a score on this scale.

Research Hypotheses

The following research hypotheses were tested according to the statistical analyses indicated within each hypothesis as listed below.

Hypothesis One. Is there a difference between Hispanic American and European American Just World Beliefs? The hypothesis pertaining to this question is as follows and was statistically tested using the t-test:

1. The population of Hispanic Americans will have lower Just World Beliefs than the population of European Americans.

Hypothesis Two. Is there a difference between European Americans and Hispanic Americans in their attitudes toward the sentencing of criminal defendants found guilty, regardless of ethnicity? The hypothesis pertaining to this question is as follows and was statistically tested using the t-test:

2. The population of Hispanic Americans will give more lenient sentences than the population of European Americans.

Hypothesis Three. Is there an interaction between the juror's ethnicity and the defendant's ethnicity concerning findings of guilt and punitiveness of sentence? The hypothesis pertaining to this question is as follows and was statistically tested using analysis of variance (ANOVA).

3. For the population of people acting as jurors, the mean (length of sentence) for criminal defendants of a different ethnicity will be greater than for defendants of the same ethnicity.

Hypothesis Four. What function does the ethnicity of the juror, the ethnicity of the defendant, and the juror's just world beliefs, play in juror bias toward criminal defendants? The hypothesis pertaining to this question is as follows and was statistically tested using multiple linear regression.

4. Jurors' just world belief scores will be significantly predictive of ATPC over and above the variables of ethnicity of the juror, and ethnicity of the defendant.

Hypothesis Five. Is there a relationship between a juror's just world beliefs and length of sentence chosen for a criminal defendant? The hypothesis pertaining to this question is as follows and was statistically tested using Spearman correlation.

5. For the population of people acting as jurors, Just World Beliefs will be positively correlated to punitiveness (length) of sentencing.

Hypothesis Six. Is there a relationship between a juror's just world beliefs and their attitudes toward the punishment of criminals? The hypothesis pertaining to this question is as follows and was statistically tested using Spearman correlation.

6. For the population of people acting as jurors, Just World Beliefs will be positively correlated with scores on the Attitudes Toward Criminals Scale.

Hypothesis Seven. Is there a relationship between a juror's attitudes toward the punishment of criminals and length of sentence chosen for a criminal defendant? The hypothesis pertaining to this question is as follows and was statistically tested using Spearman correlation.

7. For the population of people acting as jurors, Attitudes Toward the Punishment of Criminal scores will be positively correlated to punitiveness (length) of sentencing.

Analysis of the Data

Research hypotheses numbers one and two were tested using t-tests while research hypothesis number three was tested using ANOVA. Research hypothesis number four was tested using multiple linear regression and research hypotheses numbers five through seven were tested using Spearman correlation.

Assumptions of the Study

It is assumed, based on the literature that racial bias within the criminal justice system does occur. It is also assumed that ethnicity plays a role both within the jury system and against potential defendants because of individual ethnic or cultural beliefs, and stereotypes.

Some of these beliefs, such as just world beliefs, may contribute to negative attitudes toward a defendant based upon the notion that "one gets what he or she deserves." While these beliefs have been studied extensively in attitudes toward victims, very few have looked at how jury member's just world beliefs may play a role in verdicts of guilty or innocent or sentencing length. It is assumed that just world beliefs would play a similar role in how a jury member looks at a defendant as he or she does when looking at a victim of a crime.

Delimitations

Any person over the age of 18 can be a potential jury member. Therefore the participant population is vast. The sample selected for this study came from university graduate and undergraduate students from a variety of majors. This delimits the study in that participants may have more education and be younger than the general population.

In addition, there is a group dynamic that can be created when a jury of peers meets to deliberate the evidence in a trial. Since the jurors in this study do not have benefit of that process, and are making decisions alone, this may delimit the study and the findings may not be generalizable to a jury composed of members greater than one. Furthermore, participants have been limited to the ethnicities of European American and Hispanic American.

Summary

Because researchers do not have access to the jury deliberation room or process there has been primarily two methods for studying jury decision-making: Archival analyses and mock jury experiments. Since real juries cannot be manipulated or studied except ex post facto a mock jury study is the best solution for researchers wishing to explain jury bias. This study utilizes the method of using the mock jury, specifically mock jurors.

A case vignette in which the ethnicity of the defendant was randomly assigned was given to each participant. Participants were asked to read the case vignette and assign a sentence they felt was fair and just for the crime using the Juror Decision Record. Participants were also asked to fill out a demographic sheet, the Just World Beliefs Scale (Rubin & Peplau, 1975), and the Attitude Toward the Punishment of Criminals Scale (Wang & Thurstone, 1931 as cited by Shaw & Wright, 1967).

Seven hypotheses were stated. Three hypotheses addressed ethnic differences in just world beliefs, attitudes toward the punishment of criminals, and punitiveness (length) of sentencing. One hypothesis looked at the salience of the ethnicity of the juror, the ethnicity of the defendant, and the juror's just world beliefs in the phenomenon of juror bias. The last three hypotheses looked at the relationships between just world beliefs and punitiveness (length) of sentencing, just world beliefs and juror's attitudes toward the punishment of criminals, and juror's attitudes toward the punishment of criminals and punitiveness (length) of sentencing.

CHAPTER FOUR
Results

The current study was interested in examining how the ethnicity of the juror, the ethnicity of the defendant, the juror's attitudes toward the punishment of criminals, and the juror's just world beliefs impacted a juror in his or her decision regarding the punitiveness (length) of sentence established for a guilty criminal defendant. The current study used the Just World Belief Scale, the Attitudes Toward the Punishment of Criminals Scale, the Juror Decision Record, and a demographic sheet whereby participants selected the ethnicity they felt best represented them. The Chronbach's alpha for the Just World Belief Scale with this sample was (r = 0.63) and the Chronbach's alpha for the Attitude Toward the Punishment of Criminals Scale was (r = 0.70). Each participant was also given a random stimulus of a criminal case in which all the details of the defendant remained constant except for the ethnicity of the criminal defendant, which was manipulated between the ethnicities of European American, Hispanic American, and African American. This chapter discusses participant demographics and the results of the seven research hypotheses presented.

Hypothesis One

The Just World Belief scale was used to ascertain if there was a difference between European Americans and Hispanic Americans in regard to whether they believed the world was essentially a just place. The hypothesis "The population of Hispanic Americans will have lower Just World Belief scores than the population of European Americans" was tested using the t-test and was not significant. The means of the two groups were not significantly different for the samples of European American (M = 3.43, SD = 0.50) and Hispanic American (M = 3.52, SD = 0.40), t (88) = - 0.94, p = 0.35 (one-tailed).

Hypothesis Two

The Attitudes Toward the Punishment of Criminals scale was used to determine if there was a difference between European Americans and Hispanic Americans regarding their attitudes toward the punishment of a criminal defendant found guilty. The hypothesis "the population of Hispanic Americans will have more lenient attitudes toward the punishment of criminals than the population of European Americans" was tested using the t-test and was not significant. The means of the two groups were not significantly different for the samples of European American (*M* = 10.65, *SD* = 8.82) and Hispanic American (M = 8.50, *SD* = 9.36), t (88) = 1.23, p = 0.27 (one-tailed).

Hypothesis Three

Participants were asked to choose the ethnicity with which they most identified and this information along with the juror decision record was used to determine if there were differences between the punitiveness (length) of sentence given for a criminal defendant of a different ethnicity than the juror. The hypothesis "for the population of people acting as jurors, the mean frequency for punitiveness (length of sentence) for criminal defendants of a different ethnicity is greater than for defendants of the same ethnicity" was tested using an ANOVA and the result was not significant F (5, 89) = 0.45, p = 0.81.

The means and standard deviations for the groups were European American juror and European American defendant (*M* = 10.77, *SD* = 8.04), European American juror and Hispanic American defendant) (*M* = 11.76, *SD* = 10.87), European American juror and African American defendant (*M* = 8.60, *SD* = 5.82), Hispanic American juror and European American defendant (*M* = 8.07, *SD* = 6.34), Hispanic American juror and Hispanic American defendant (*M* = 9.42, *SD* =11.06), and Hispanic American juror and African American defendant (*M* = 7.82, *SD* = 9.82). These groups were then analyzed in terms of similar vs. dissimilar (e.g., same ethnicity of juror and defendant) vs. (different ethnicity of juror and defendant). These results were also not statistically significant F (1) = 0.24, p = 0.62.

Hypothesis Four

A model was predicted to have salience in the prediction of juror bias as measured by the Attitudes Toward the Punishment of Criminals Scale. It was hypothesized that a juror's ethnicity, his or her just world beliefs, and the defendant's ethnicity would predict juror scores on the ATPC scale. This model was tested using multiple linear regression. The test of the entire model was not significant F (4, 85) = 2.39, p = .053, r2 = .10 (see table 3). The variables of just world belief scores, ethnicity of the juror, and ethnicity of the defendant were not significant predictors of a participant's Attitudes Toward the Punishment of Criminals scale scores, although the alpha approached significance.

The researcher was also interested in ascertaining which of the variables under study impacted a juror's potential to be biased toward a criminal defendant the most out of all the variables under study. The hypothesis "juror bias is a function of the juror's just world beliefs over and above the variables of ethnicity of the juror and ethnicity of the defendant" was tested also using multiple linear regression. The participants' scores on the Just World Beliefs scale, the ethnicity of the juror, and random assignment of the stimulus, which manipulated the ethnicity of the criminal defendant were all used in the equation as independent variables with the dependent variable of Attitudes Toward the Punishment of Criminals scale. The hypothesis was not significant as stated. A juror's Just World Belief scores were not found to be a significant predictor of bias toward a criminal defendant over and above the variables of ethnicity of the juror and ethnicity of the defendant, F (1) = 0.31, p = 0.58, (one-tailed). The ethnicity of the juror as a predictor was also not significant, F (1) = 1.01, p = 0.32, but the random assignment of the ethnicity of the defendant, F (2) = 4.12, p = 0.01 was statistically significant (see Table 4). However, since the entire model was not found to be significant, this finding while interesting needs further exploration and replication.

Table 3

Regression Predicting Attitudes Toward the Punishment of Criminals Scale

Source	*SS*	*df*	*MS*	*F*	*p*
Model	6110.02593	4	1527.50648	2.39	0.0572*
Error	54354.91195	85	639.46955		
Corrected Total	60464.93789	89			

*p = > .05.

Participants were randomly assigned the ethnicity of the defendant; 30% (n = 27) of participants received a European American defendant, 40% (n = 36) received a Hispanic American defendant, and 30% (n = 27) received a African American defendant. The mean scores on the ATPC scale for participants with a European American defendant were (M =

79.04, *SD* = 27.60), for a Hispanic American defendant (*M* = 62.59, *SD* = 30.82), and for a African American Defendant (*M* = 62.75, *SD* = 17.52).

Table 4

Results for Random Assignment

Source	*df*	*F*	*p*
Juror Ethnicity	1	1.01	0.3168
Defendant Ethnicity	2	4.12	0.0196*
Just World Belief Scores	1	0.31	0.5820

*$p < .05$.

Hypothesis Five

The researcher was also interested in evaluating whether or not a juror's just world beliefs was related to his or her ultimate decision in terms of sentencing length for a criminal defendant. The Just World Belief scale scores and the juror's decision record were used with the hypothesis "for the population of people acting as jurors, Just World Beliefs are positively correlated to punitiveness (length) of sentencing." This hypothesis was tested using Spearman correlation. The results were $r = .01$, $p = 0.94$. This was not significant.

Hypothesis Six

In addition, the researcher wanted to know if there was a relationship between a juror's just world beliefs and his or her attitudes toward the punishment of criminals. The participant's Just World Belief scale score and his or her Attitudes Toward the Punishment of Criminals score was used to test the hypothesis "for the population of people acting as jurors, Just World Beliefs are positively correlated with scores on the Attitudes Toward Criminals Scale." This hypothesis was tested using Spearman correlation. The results of this test was $r = .06$, $p = 0.55$. This hypothesis was not statistically significant.

Hypothesis Seven

The last research question for this study was "is there a relationship between a juror's attitudes toward the punishment of criminals and length of sentence chosen for a criminal defendant?" Participant's Attitude Toward the Punishment of Criminals scores and their decision records were used to test the hypothesis "for the population of people acting as jurors, Attitudes Toward the Punishment of Criminal scores are positively correlated to punitiveness (length) of sentencing." This hypothesis was tested using Spearman correlation. The results were $r = .11$, $p = 0.32$. This hypothesis was not significant. The range of scores for sentencing was 01 – 36 and the mean was 07.

Summary

Seven hypotheses were tested for this study and none were found significant. Just world beliefs as a predictor of juror bias as measured by the Attitudes Toward the Punishment of Criminals Scale was not found significant. However, there was an interesting finding. The results indicated that among the variables of juror's just world beliefs, the ethnicity of the juror, and the ethnicity of the defendant, the random assignment of the ethnicity of the defendant was a salient predictor and participants held significantly more juror bias toward European American defendants as measured by the Attitudes Toward the Punishment of Criminals scale. These results bear more investigation.

CHAPTER FIVE
Discussion

This section provides a review and discussion of the results of the seven hypotheses presented in relationship to the literature and the importance of the findings. In addition, a discussion as to the current study's relevance to the field of counseling psychology and suggestions for future research is provided.

Summary of the Purpose

Whenever the proportion of minorities processed through the criminal justice system exceeds the proportion such groups represent in the general population, racial disparity is said to exist (Davies, 2003; Reducing Racial Disparity, 2007). As of 2005, 66% of the inmates in U.S. prisons and jails were of minority status (Facts About Prisoners and Prisons, 2007; International Center for Prison Studies, 2007; Reducing Racial Disparity, 2007).

The prison population of the U.S. is steadily increasing and along with that general increase is a higher number of minority individuals who will spend time behind bars disproportionately to the European American population (Bureau of Justice Statistics, 2002a, 2002b, 2006; Davies, 2003; Facts about Prisoners and Prisons, 2007; Luna, 2003; Morgan et al., 2007; Platt, 2001; Reducing Racial Disparity, 2007; Sorensen et al., 2003).

This issue is growing in saliency because the population of incarcerated individuals is growing exponentially. Since the 1980s, the state and federal prison population in this country has grown by 400% - 600% and there has been a steady increase in the number of inmates housed in U.S. jails and prisons for the last 33 years despite the fact that the overall crime rate has gone down (Bureau of Justice Statistics, 2002b, 2006; Facts about Prisoners and Prisons, 2007; New Incarceration Figures, 2006). Therefore the issue of racial disparity within the U.S. prison population is expected to increase (Reducing Racial Disparity, 2007).

While many studies have documented bias within the criminal justice system research has not been able to account for the discrepancies between minority and European American individual incarceration rates, or sentence length, even for the same crimes committed. Several theories have been proposed, however no concrete explanation has been found regarding the inherent differences in treatment of persons from minority groups (e.g., African

American, Hispanic American) in comparison to the majority ethnic group (e.g., European American) when looking at juror bias and how that affects sentence length.

The current study was interested in examining how the ethnicity of the juror, the ethnicity of the defendant, the juror's just world beliefs, and the juror's attitudes toward the punishment of criminals impacted a juror in his or her verdict regarding the length of sentence established for a guilty criminal defendant. Participants were asked to read a case vignette of an individual found guilty of a crime in which the variable of ethnicity of the defendant was manipulated between the ethnicities of European American, Hispanic American, and African American. They were also asked to choose the ethnicity in which they most identified and fill out a demographic sheet, the Just World Belief scale, and the Attitudes Toward the Punishment of Criminals scale.

Ethnic Differences in Just World Beliefs

The first research question explored was whether there was a difference between European American and Hispanic American mock juror participants' just world beliefs? The ethnic self-identification of participants and their Just World Belief Scale scores were used to test the hypothesis "The population of Hispanic Americans will have lower Just World Belief scores than the population of European Americans" using the t-test. This hypothesis was not significant. The score range for the Just World Belief scale is 1 (total rejection of just world beliefs) to 6 (total acceptance of Just World Beliefs). The means of the two groups were European American (M = 3.43, SD = 0.50) and Hispanic American (M = 3.52, SD = 0.40), t (88) = - 0.94, p = 0.35 (one-tailed). Both groups held moderate beliefs that the world was just. There were no statistical differences found between Hispanic Americans and European Americans in their belief in a just world within this participant population. Therefore, this study did not support the supposition and findings of other studies that just world beliefs is a cultural variable and that different ethnicities should have different beliefs that the world is just (Furnham, 1991a, 1991b; Hunt, 2000; Lambert & Raichle, 2000).

Some theorists consider that belief in a just world is a cultural variable and a part of a person's worldview and people of different ethnicities should have variations regarding this belief based upon culture (Hunt, 2000; Lambert & Raichle, 2000). Furnham & Proctor (1989) theorized that as children grow into adults their beliefs that the world is just and "people deserve what they get" are reinforced or disputed by their personal experiences. For example, those individuals who have been discriminated against because of racism, have been victims of crime, or have experienced other unjustness, probably would eventually refute the idea that the world is a just place. In fact, it is considered that two of the most important factors in terms of belief in just world is the participant's own experiences with injustice and his or her own race (Furnham & Proctor; Hunt, 2000). Hunt (2000) when comparing European American, African American, and Hispanic American participants on just world beliefs using the same Rubin and Peplau Just World Belief scale found significant differences between three ethnic groups. The current study did not support this finding.

One possible explanation for why there may not have been a difference between Hispanic American and European American beliefs that the world is just could be due to the nature of this particular sample population. This sample of participants was selected from a university located in a region with a high population of Hispanic Americans. Therefore, experiences due to racism, discrimination, or oppression might not be as salient in this population as it might be in other populations where Hispanic American culture is not so prominent.

It could also be that within this region where Hispanic American culture is prominent that many European American's have felt discriminated against, or felt they were the victims of bias, in ways similar to how Hispanic Americans typically might feel when they live in regions that are more predominately European American. This might also lead to European Americans having similar beliefs regarding the justness of the world in this sample of participants. More research is needed regarding variables that impact an individual's belief in a just world and how experiences of racism, oppression, discrimination, and contact with the criminal justice system play a role in such beliefs. In addition, reading a case vignette whereby the defendant was convicted on circumstantial evidence prior to filling out this scale may have impacted participants' scores on the JWB scale. It may have influenced them to believe the world is less just then they might have otherwise have concluded.

Rubin and Peplau (1975) hypothesized that individuals who have experienced injustice will have lower just world beliefs. Research indicates that younger females who are lower on the gender hierarchy (e.g., have less social status due to gender socialization) have lower just world beliefs than males (Hunt, 2000; Lipkus et al., 1996). The high number of young women in this study may have impacted the outcome in variation on this scale. Subsequently, the JWB scale also had low reliability for this population, which further may have impacted scores.

In addition, the overall socioeconomic status (SES) of participants was moderately high. Seventy-three percent of participants belonged to the SES category II and III as identified by the Hollingshead Two Factor Index of Social Position (Miller, 1983). Those individuals from a higher SES may not have experienced as much discrimination or other factors that might impact their beliefs in a just world as opposed to individuals from a lower SES status. Research indicates that individuals from lower SES statuses have lower just world beliefs (Hunt, 2000). The relative high SES status among this participant sample may also have impacted this group of participant's JWB scores.

Ethnic Differences in Attitudes Toward Punishment

The second research question explored whether there was a difference between European American and Hispanic American mock jurors in their attitudes toward the punishment of criminals. The ethnic self-identification of the participant from the demographic sheet and the Attitudes Toward the Punishment of Criminals scale was used to determine if there was a difference between European Americans and Hispanic Americans regarding their attitudes toward the punishment of a criminal defendant found guilty. The hypothesis "the population of Hispanic Americans will have more lenient attitudes toward the punishment of criminals than will the population of European Americans," was tested using the t-test and was not significant. For this study, there was no statistical difference between Hispanic American and European American participants in terms of their attitudes toward the punishment of a criminal defendant. Therefore, this study did not find that Hispanic Americans and European Americans differed in their attitudes toward the punishment of criminals.

The Attitude Toward the Punishment of Criminals scale possible score range was 0 (if no items were endorsed) to 186.2 (if all items are endorsed). High scores indicate a punitive attitude toward the punishment of criminals whereas low scores indicate a lenient attitude. The results for this study showed the means of the two groups were European American (M = 10.65, SD = 8.82) and Hispanic American (M = 8.50, SD = 9.36), t (88) = 1.23, p = 0.27 (one-tailed). Therefore, both groups had relatively lenient attitudes toward the punishment of criminals. The current study did not support either of the hypotheses presented by different groups of researchers that:

(a) Minority jurors would be more lenient toward other minority defendants (Broeder, 1959; Crocker et al., 1994; Dane & Wrightsman, 1982; Enomoto, 1999; Johnson et al., 2002; King, 1993; Montada, 1998; Murray et al., 1997; Sellers et al., 1998; Smith, 1991; Valk & Karu, 2001; Verkuyten, 2003; Wuensch et al., 2002; Yueh-Ting & Ottati, 2002).

(b) Minority jurors would be more punitive toward other minority defendants (King, 1993; Miller & Hewitt, 1978).

The majority of research supports the notion that minorities are given longer and more punitive sentences than European Americans for the same type of crime. This has been found true even though European Americans and ethnic minorities have essentially the same crime commission and recidivism rates (Alvarez & Bachman, 1996; Camp, 1994; Crawford, 2000; Facts About Prisoners and Prisons, 2007; Free, 1997; Gastwirth & Nayak, 1997; Glasser, 2000; International Center For Prison Studies, 2007; New York Study, 1996; Petersilia, 1983; Reducing Racial Disparity, 2007; Spohn & Holleran, 2000; Steffensmeier & Demuth, 2001). Research is mixed as to whether an individual who is of an ethnic minority status would have more lenient attitudes toward the punishment of another minority individual. Some research implies that a minority juror (e.g., Hispanic American) might be more lenient toward a minority criminal defendant, especially to a Hispanic American defendant, and therefore would be more lenient in recommendations of punishment for that defendant. This is thought to be due to the shared experiences of ethnic bias, shared experiences with racism, discrimination, and oppression, and from the psychological need to maintain a positive self-image (Broeder, 1959; Crocker et al., 1994; Dane & Wrightsman, 1982; Enomoto, 1999; Johnson et al., 2002; King, 1993; Montada, 1998; Murray, Kaiser et al., 1997; Sellers et al., 1998; Smith, 1991; Valk & Karu, 2001; Verkuyten, 2003; Wuensch et al., 2002; Yueh-Ting & Ottati, 2002).

It is well known that ethnic minorities are disproportionately affected by the criminal justice system (Bureau of Justice Statistics, 2002a, 2002b, 2002c, 2002e, 2006). Therefore, odds are also increased for a member of one of these populations to have either been incarcerated, or else have a close friend or family member who has been incarcerated, which may also impact their attitudes toward the punishment of a minority criminal defendant.

However, multicultural theory and other research suggest a person from a collectivist society (e.g., Hispanic Americans) might be harsher in their attitudes toward another individual of his or her ethnicity (King, 1993; Miller & Hewitt, 1978). This is thought to be because the defendant's actions (e.g., commission of a crime) can be seen as a betrayal because collectivist societies work together for the advancement and welfare of the group, and value cooperation. Collectivism (e.g., Hispanic American culture), unlike individualism (e.g., European American culture), holds the group as the primary entity and sets the standard of moral value over and above that of the individual (Sue & Sue, 1999). With regard to crime and criminal defendants, people in collectivist societies might view a defendant from their group as having let down the community and be more punitive toward that individual.

One possible explanation for the lack of difference between Hispanic American and European Americans in this population is that the European American participants in this study are living in a high population of Hispanic Americans. Abwender and Hough (2001) noted in their study that on the basis of previous research, sometimes European American participants will "bend over backwards" to appear unprejudiced. If this is so, then some European American participants might make different decisions toward ethnic minority defendants in order to appear non-racist. So there could be a social desirability effect in this current research that might cause this group of European American participants to hold more lenient attitudes toward African American and Hispanic American criminal defendants.

Acculturation might also have played a role in the results of this study. Many of the Hispanic American individuals, even though they retain much of their Hispanic American cultural heritage, are also bi-cultural and many have lived all their lives in the U.S. This may cause them to hold similar views to European Americans regarding many issues such as crime and punishment. In this manner, acculturation can have a moderating effect on ethnic differences between participant jurors. Since an acculturation measure was not used it is impossible to ascertain what effects, if any, acculturation had on the results of this study.

In addition there could be a sex effect occurring as the majority of this participant sample (91%) was female. Sex and gender can also play a role in how one perceives defendants and crime. As mentioned, boys and girls are socialized to play different roles within society (Berndt, 1997). Therefore, it could be hypothesized based upon stereotypical gender socialization that females would have more lenient attitudes toward criminal defendants than would males (Wuensch et al., 2002).

This may be especially true for cultures with more rigid gender role schemata such as the Hispanic American culture. For example, a Hispanic American female may hold different views than a Hispanic American male due to gender role socialization. It has been hypothesized that the racial variations in employment and family patterns may cause ethnic minorities (e.g., Hispanic Americans) to hold more traditional gender-related attitudes than do European Americans (Eisenman & Dantzker, 2006; McGoldrick et al., 1996). The effect between culture and gender in this sample of participants, as well as the other variables mentioned, might have impacted the results of this study and are possible explainers of why the hypothesis that Hispanic American participants would give more lenient sentences over all was not supported in this study.

Ethnic Differences in Sentencing Length

The third research question explored was whether mock juror participants would give longer sentences to those criminal defendants who were ethically different from them. Participants were asked to choose the ethnicity with which they most identified and this information along with the juror decision record for sentencing was used to determine if there were differences between the punitiveness (e.g., length) of sentence given in months for different ethnic defendants. Participants had the option of choosing zero months (e.g., probation only and no jail time) to up to 36 months of incarceration for the offence. This sentencing variation was chosen because it represented the real time consequence in the state in which this study took place for the particular crime represented in the case vignette.

The hypothesis "for the population of people acting as jurors, the mean frequency for punitiveness (length of sentence) for criminal defendants of a different ethnicity is greater than for defendants of the same ethnicity" was tested using the t-test and the result was not statistically significant F (5, 84) = .45, p = .81 (one-tailed test). Initially, an ANOVA was conducted for each of the sub-groups (e.g., European American juror – European American defendant; European American juror – Hispanic American defendant; European American juror – African American defendant, Hispanic American juror – Hispanic American defendant; Hispanic American juror – Hispanic American juror – European American defendant, and

Hispanic American juror – African American defendant). Further analysis for this hypothesis looked at these groups as "similars" versus "dissimilars" (e.g., same ethnicity of juror and defendant) vs. (different ethnicity of juror and defendant). There was again, no statistical difference in this sample $F(1) = .24$, $p = .62$ (one-tailed test).

Therefore, research that implies a minority juror who is the same ethnicity as the defendant would be more lenient in recommended sentencing of that defendant was not supported in this analysis for this population (Broeder, 1959; Crocker et al., 1994; Dane & Wrightsman, 1982; Enomoto, 1999; Johnson et al., 2002; King, 1993; Montada, 1998; Murray et al., 1997; Sellers et al., 1998; Smith, 1991; Valk & Karu, 2001; Verkuyten, 2003; Wuensch et al., 2002; Yueh-Ting & Ottati, 2002).

In addition, while the majority of research and statistics supporting the notion that minorities are given longer and harsher sentences than European Americans for the same type of crime, this was also not supported in this study for this sample (Bureau of Justice Statistics, 2006; Alvarez & Bachman, 1996; Camp, 1994; Crawford, 2000; Free, 1997; Gastwirth & Nayak, 1997; Glasser, 2000; Landwehr et al., 2002; Levin et al., 2000; Matthews, 2000; McDonald & Carlson, 1993; New York Study, 1996; Petersilia, 1983; Spohn & Holleran, 2000; Steffensmeier & Demuth, 2001; Unnever et al., 1980; U.S. Sentencing Commission, 1991).

Other research studies have indicated a pattern that suggests defendants may receive longer sentences when they are convicted of crimes that are stereotypically associated with their ethnicity (Bodenhausen & Wyer, 1985; Gordon, 1990; Gordon et al., 1988; Hurwitz & Peffley, 1997; Mazella & Feingold, 1994; Wuensch et al., 2002). The crime in the case vignette for this study depicted a robbery of convenience of tools from an open garage in which the evidence was largely circumstantial, yet the defendant was found guilty. Some participants may have associated crimes of this type to be stereotypically more likely in one ethnicity over another. It is unknown to this researcher how these ethnic populations are viewed in terms of theft in the region where this study was conducted.

Predictor of Juror Bias

The fourth research question explored the function of the different variables under exploration in terms of their relation to juror bias as measured by the Attitudes Toward the

Punishment of Criminals Scale. It was hypothesized that a juror's just world beliefs would be more salient in contributing to juror bias than the variables of ethnicity of the juror or the ethnicity of the criminal defendant. Participants' Just World Belief score averages, the ethnicity of the participants, and the random assignment of the ethnicity of the defendants were used as independent variables with participants' scores on the Attitudes Toward the Punishment of Criminals Scale as the dependent variable. The hypothesis "juror bias is a function of the juror's just world beliefs over and above the variables of ethnicity of the juror and ethnicity of the defendant was tested using multiple linear regression. The test of the entire model as a predictor of the participant's score on the Attitude Toward the Punishment of Criminals scale score only approached significance, F (4, 85) = 2.39, p = .053, (one-tailed test). The model predicted 10% of the variance in ATPC scores.

The analysis of the individual variables of a participant's just world belief scores, ethnicity of the juror, and the random assignment of the ethnicity of the defendant did not support the hypothesis that the juror's just world beliefs would be the most salient predictor of juror bias as measured by the ATPC scale. Participant beliefs in a just world as a factor in their Attitudes Toward the Punishment of Criminals scores F (1) =2.39, p = 0.58 (one-tailed test), was not significant. Nor was the ethnicity of the participant F (1) = 1.01, p = 0.32. The results of this study with this group of participants did not significantly support the results of other studies that suggest just world beliefs plays a larger role in juror bias. When looking at this participant sample's Just World Belief scores, the European American and Hispanic American scores were not statistically different (M = 3.43, SD = 0.50) and Hispanic American (M = 3.52, SD = 0.40), t (88) = 0.94, p = 0.35. As mentioned, the JWB scale uses a total score with a range from 1 (represents a total rejection of just world beliefs) to 6 (represents a total acceptance of just world beliefs). This sample of participants overall had moderate beliefs in a just world, which may have impacted this hypothesis. Had these participants had more variation in their just world beliefs a more salient role of just world beliefs in relationship to sentencing might have been found.

However, what emerged from the data as an interesting finding related to juror bias in this current study was the random assignment of the ethnicity of the criminal defendant, F (2) = 4.12, p = .01. Participants who had a European American defendant 40% (n = 36), held significantly more punitive attitudes toward the punishment of criminals as measured by the

Attitudes Toward the Punishment of Criminals Scale (ATPC) (*M* = 79.04, *SD* = 27.60), than either participants who had a Hispanic American defendant 30% (*n* = 27), (*M* = 62.59, *SD* = 30.82), or participants who had a African American defendant 30% (*n* = 27), (*M* = 62.75, *SD* = 17.52). This finding needs further investigation since the entire model was not found to be significant.

As mentioned, the total possible score range for the ATPC scale was 0 – 186 with higher numbers indicating more punitive attitudes toward the punishment of criminals. However, while participants with European American defendants held more punitive attitudes toward the punishment of criminals, this punitive attitude did not result in significantly longer sentences for European American defendants. When looking at sentence length assigned to the defendants, European Americans were given average sentences of (*M* = 9.37 months, *SD* = 7.20), Hispanic Americans (*M* = 10.53 months, *SD* = 10.88), and African Americans (*M* = 8.11 months, *SD* = 8.44). These differences were not statistically significant.

Therefore, while there seemed to be more punitive attitudes toward the punishment of criminals exhibited by jurors with European American defendants as measured by the ATPC scale, this did not translate into longer, more punitive, sentences for European American defendants. So while there may have been a covert bias (attitudes) it did not transform into an overt bias (sentence length). The results of the current study contradicts the Bureau of Justice Statistics and research that indicate that there is more bias toward minority defendants than European American defendants within the criminal justice system (Alvarez & Bachman, 1996; Bureau of Justice Statistics, 2006; Camp, 1994; Crawford, 2000; Free, 1997; Gastwirth & Nayak, 1997; Glasser, 2000; Heaney, 1991; New York Study, 1996; Petersilia, 1983; Spohn & Holleran, 2000; Steffensmeier & Demuth, 2001).

The results of this study also do not support research that suggests just world beliefs contribute to juror bias. O'Quin and Vogler (1989) pointed out that very little attention has been given to punishment reactions or reactions toward defendants of crime within just world belief research. This has remained true in the ensuing years and has been an area overlooked in the research literature. The focus of this study was to contribute to research that supported the hypothesis that just world beliefs might play a role in juror bias toward criminal defendant sentencing. Of those few studies that have looked at defendants of crime, several have found support that just world beliefs play a role in defendant sentencing (Finamore & Carlson, 1987; Lambert & Raichle, 2000; Lerner, 1980; Rubin and Peplau, 1975).

For example, Finamore and Carlson (1987) found that high beliefs in a just world are related to crime control attitudes. They found high just world beliefs related to an assumption that the defendant was guilty and the belief that the police make few mistakes, and therefore, no sympathy should be wasted on those accused of a crime. Lerner (1980) found that jurors with high just world beliefs have been more likely to give harsher sentences to defendants accused of heinous crimes such as negligent homicide. Rubin and Peplau's (1975) research suggested that when the defendant directly caused a victim's suffering, then the juror with high just world beliefs would seek to restore justice for the victim.

However, the results of the current study may support Lambert and Raichle's (2000) study, which stated that verdicts of guilt and sentencing length are often determined by individual judgments of personal blame and that despite having the exact same evidence; perceivers come to different conclusions. All of the details in the case vignette for the current study were exactly the same except for the random assignment of the ethnicity of the criminal defendant. Participants who had European American defendants exhibited significantly more juror bias as measured by the Attitudes Toward the Punishment of Criminals scale than either Hispanic American or African Americans defendants.

<u>The Relationship of Just World Beliefs and Sentencing Length</u>

The fifth research question explored the relationship between a juror's just world beliefs and the length of sentence chosen for a criminal defendant. It was hypothesized that there would be a positive correlation between a juror's just world beliefs and the length of sentence he or she chose. Therefore the jurors with high just world beliefs would hold firm notions that bad things didn't happen to good people and if a criminal defendant was found guilty then he or she probably was. It was hypothesized that the juror would then be more likely to assign a long sentence than someone with low just world beliefs.

Participants' Just World Belief scale scores and the juror decision record were used to test this hypothesis using Spearman correlation. The hypothesis "For the population of people acting as jurors, just world beliefs are positively correlated to punitiveness (length) of sentencing" was not significant ($r = .00$, $p = 0.94$).

This was an unexpected finding and did not support Finamore and Carlson's (1987) findings. Finamore and Carlson found that high beliefs in a just world are related to crime control attitudes and related to an assumption that the defendant was guilty; the belief that the police make few mistakes, and therefore, a criminal defendant was probably guilty of the crime for which he or she was accused. As mentioned, the participants in this study had moderate just world belief scores. Therefore, participant just world beliefs may not have been high enough to impact sentence length in this sample.

Lerner (1980) found that jurors with high just world beliefs have been more likely to give harsher sentences to defendants accused of heinous crimes such as negligent homicide. These findings may not hold as true for criminals accused or convicted of lesser crimes such as theft. The vignette in this study depicted a case of felony theft whereby the defendant was convicted on largely circumstantial evidence. This may have impacted the results for this study based on previous research. Future research may need to use a vignette in which the crime is more heinous or at least less ambiguous. In addition, the JWB scale had low reliability with this participant sample. This also may have impacted the results of this study.

Rubin and Peplau's (1975) research suggests that when it was perceived that the defendant directly caused a victim's suffering then the juror with high just world beliefs would seek to restore justice for the victim (e.g., assign a more punitive sentence). The circumstantial evidence of the case vignette in this study may have made it difficult for participants to assess if the defendant caused the victim suffering or that it was intentional on the part of the defendant.

Relationship of Just World Beliefs and Attitudes Toward Punishment

The sixth research question explored the relationship between a juror's just world beliefs and his or her attitudes toward the punishment of criminals. It was hypothesized that a mock juror's scores on the Just World Belief Scale would be positively correlated with their scores on the Attitudes Toward the Punishment of Criminals scale. Therefore, those jurors with high just world beliefs would hold more punitive attitudes toward the punishment of criminals rather than someone with low just world beliefs.

Participants' Just World Belief scale scores and their Attitudes Toward the Punishment of Criminals scores were used to test the hypothesis "For the population of people acting as jurors, Just World Beliefs are positively correlated with scores on the Attitudes Toward Criminals Scale" using Spearman correlation. This hypothesis was not significant, $r = .06$, $p = 0.55$. This study did not find just world beliefs to be correlated to punitive attitudes toward the punishment of criminals. Therefore, within this sample whether a juror had high or low just world beliefs did not impact the choices he or she made in recommending a sentence for the criminal defendant in the vignette. There is no research that explores the relationship between just world beliefs and attitudes toward the punishment of criminals.

Relationship Between Attitudes Toward Punishment and Sentencing

The last research question explored was whether there was a relationship between a mock juror's attitudes toward the punishment of criminals and the length of sentence chosen for a criminal defendant. Therefore, those mock juror's who scored high (punitive) on the Attitude Toward the Punishment of Criminals scale would be more likely to give longer sentences to criminal defendants than juror's who scored low on this scale.

Participants' Attitude Toward the Punishment of Criminals scores and their decision records were used to test the hypothesis "For the population of people acting as jurors, Attitudes Toward the Punishment of Criminal scores are positively correlated to punitiveness (length) of sentencing." Spearman correlation was used to test this hypothesis and it was not significant ($r = -.10$, $p = 0.32$). Therefore, in this study, participants' attitudes toward the punishment of criminals were not related to how participants sentenced a criminal defendant. There was no relationship between a juror having a punitive orientation toward the punishment of criminals and his or her choice when deciding on a sentence for the criminal defendant in the vignette. No research was found that looked at a mock juror's attitudes toward the punishment of criminals and their resulting recommendations for sentencing.

Limitations

Limitations in the present study were related to age, participant sample, geographical location, ethnic categorization, gender composition of the participants, contact with the criminal justice system, ambiguity of the case vignette, and reliability of the measures.

Age. Since this research was conducted in a university setting, one obvious limitation is age. The mean age of this participant sample was 24 with a range of 17-52. While there is much variability within this sample, the younger average age may not correspond to the mean age of the surrounding community or other communities within the U.S. Therefore, the results may not be generalizable to the greater population, which has a higher mean age. In addition, younger individuals who do not have a lot of life experience may not have had as many discriminatory or traumatic experiences and may have a higher belief in a just world than someone older.

Sample. The sample of the current study was one of convenience and participants were volunteers who self-selected. Some participants received extra credit in their classes for their participation. Their reasons for participating in this research might be different from others who could have been randomly selected. Those that volunteered might also be different in other ways from those who did not volunteer. This self-selection might have influenced the results of this study. In addition, university students are often used in research and such participants are not always reflective of the greater community population. However, due to access and time constraints a decision was made to utilize these participants.

Geographical Location. The demographical makeup within the geographical area in which this study took place is not necessarily representative of other communities, either within the U.S., or within the same state. It might be difficult to generalize the results found in this study beyond this community. The community within which these participants were drawn has a substantially higher Hispanic American population than average for the U.S. (Hispanic Americans in the U.S., 2007; Las Cruces, 2007). Due to monetary and time constraints a decision was made to conduct this research in this geographical location despite its high Hispanic American population.

Ethnic Categorization. It should also be noted that participants were asked to self-identify the ethnicity with which they most identified. This created two categories of ethnicity for this study. Therefore this study required participants who normally would identify with dual or multiple ethnicities to choose only one. The current study also required that many of the individuals in this study who might normally identify as both European American and Hispanic American had to choose between their identities for the purpose of this research. It is highly likely in the geographical area in which this study took place that many of the individuals in this study did indeed identify with both European American and Hispanic American heritage, which might also explain why there were no significant differences between these two groups on many of the measures. Due to the nature of this research, it was important to look at differences between jurors of different ethnicities and therefore a decision was made to have participants choose the ethnicity with which they most identified. If they could not choose their data was not used in these analyses.

Given that this sample was from a university, it is also likely that those individuals who identified as Hispanic American did not all descend from the same Hispanic American groups. The term Hispanic American is an umbrella term used to identify individuals from many Spanish speaking countries such as Cuba, Mexico, the Dominican Republic, El Salvador, Argentina, Peru, and many others. Their values, beliefs, worldview, religious affiliation and so forth might be very different one from another. However, the need to affiliate these individuals all into one group entitled "Hispanic American" loses much of the richness and distinct differences between these Hispanic American cultures. The same is true for those participants that identified as European American. European American is also an umbrella term used to identify individuals from many European countries (e.g., Germany, England, Ireland, and France). The same cultural nuances are lost when grouped in such a manner.

Another factor that could have impacted this study was the acculturation level of Hispanic American participants. Many of the Hispanic American individuals, even though they retain much of their Hispanic American cultural heritage, are also bi-cultural and many have lived all their lives in the U.S. This may cause them to hold similar views to European Americans.

In addition, African American participants were not used due to the low numbers of individuals representing this ethnicity on the campus where this study was conducted. However, African American participants exhibit more phenotypal differences than do Hispanic American individuals in relationship to European Americans. The exclusion of African American participants may have affected the results based upon the tenets of Scientific Racism, (also known as Genetically Deficient Model). It is hypothesized that African Americans would have lower just world beliefs than Hispanic Americans due to phenotypal characteristics because Hispanic Americans more closely resemble European Americans in skin color than do African Americans (Oppenheimer, 2001). Criminal justice statistics confirm that Hispanic Americans have lower incarceration rates and sentence lengths than do African Americans (Bureau of Justice Statistics, 2002c, 2002e, 2006; Facts about Prisoners and Prisons, 2007;

Platt, 2001). Including African American participants may have garnered more variation in Just World Belief scores.

Gender. Ninety-one percent of the participants in this study were female. Sex and gender can also play a role in how one perceives defendants and crime. Boys and girls are socialized to play different roles within society. Girls are stereotypically thought to be more nurturing, expressive, and perhaps forgiving. In contrast, boys are thought to be more aggressive, instrumental, and harsh (Berndt, 1997). Therefore, it could be hypothesized based upon stereotypical gender socialization, that females would have more lenient attitudes toward criminal defendants than would males. An experimental study conducted by Wuensch and colleagues (2002) supported this notion.

Juror Study vs. Jury Study: There may be a potential group dynamic that occurs when a jury of peers meets to deliberate on a sentence for a criminal defendant that would be missing within this study (Bodenhausen, 2005; Bodenhausen & Wyer, 1985). The current study had each juror working alone without benefit of peer interaction. In addition, reading about a defendant is not the same as being in a trial and seeing a live defendant. Reading a case vignette might produce different results than if the juror was in a true process. Future studies might want to consider testing these hypotheses with mock juries instead of using singular jurors and perhaps use a mock trial versus just a case vignette.

Contact with the Criminal Justice System. Previous research and hypotheses suggests that individuals who have experience with the criminal justice system will have different views of that system and should have lower beliefs in a just world (Furnham & Proctor, 1989; O'Quin & Vogler, 1989). However, given that ethnic minorities even as college students are disproportionately affected by the criminal justice system, the odds are increased for a member of one of these populations to have either been incarcerated, or else have a close friend or family member who has been incarcerated (Bureau of Justice Statistics, 2002a, 2002b, 2002c, 2002e, 2006).

Due to the nature of this study and the limitations on time and finances a decision was made not to control for this variable in order to obtain a large enough participant sample within the time constraints. This may have impacted the results if previous research and hypotheses are correct that someone who has had exposure to the criminal justice system, either directly or vicariously, positively or negatively, would have differing attitudes to the punishment of criminals and just world beliefs.

Ambiguity of the Case Vignette. The current study used a case vignette in which a criminal defendant is found guilty of a crime of convenience in the theft of construction tools from an open garage. The evidence in the vignette is largely circumstantial and this was designed purposefully to test whether a juror's just world beliefs would be salient in juror bias toward a criminal defendant. However, the ambiguity and circumstantial evidence may also have impacted this study in unknown ways.

Reliability of the Measures. The Just World Belief scale had low reliability with this particular sample of participants. This undoubtedly impacted and limited this study. In addition, the JWB scale has never before been used with a Hispanic American population, which may be one factor that contributed to the low reliability with this measure. Prior populations that have been reported to have used the JWB are Chinese, European American, and African Americans.

Implications for Counseling Psychology

Counseling psychologists play a key role in the social justice arena in terms of conducting research and advocating for the rights of others in a variety of venues including institutional practice and policy change (Tomes, 2004). Social justice work conducted by counseling psychologists includes advocating for change within the criminal justice system. The current study will help increase knowledge on how minority individuals are treated within the criminal justice system and can help educate psychologists, judges, lawyers, juries, corrections officials, and the public about the effect and impact of racism on the criminal justice process.

Advocacy, according to the American Psychological Association "focuses on expanding the recognition of psychology's scientific and professional contributions and achievements and uses these to further human welfare. Among its primary objectives is the enhancement of federal support for psychological research and practice, and the application of psychological research to inform policy aimed at addressing public interest issues" (pg. 1) (Calkins, 1995).

The current study, and others like it, can be used to help inform and change policy regarding the jury system in the U.S. and highlight areas where change might be needed to include fairer practices that do not discriminate against individuals of color. For example, research has shown that bias does occur in the jury process and recently the New Jersey Administrative Office of the Court has adopted a new set of standards for jury selection based upon a model proposed by U.S. Supreme Court (Brennan, 2006). Therefore, currently in New Jersey, "the method chosen to conduct voir dire must assure a thorough and meaningful inquiry into jurors' relevant attitudes so the court and counsel can identify jurors who may possess a bias, prejudice, or unfairness with regard to the trial matter or anyone involved in the trial," (p. 1).

The increasing number of incarcerated criminal offenders, combined with growing mental health issues within the criminal justice system, will increase the need for counseling psychologists to work with offender populations (Morgan et al., 2007). In addition, the high rate of incarcerated individuals in turn leads to a high rate of individuals who will need help during their post-prison release, which compounds the need for counseling psychologists to be aware of issues facing this underserved population.

The high rate of minority offenders in comparison with European American offenders could likely cause assumptions to be made about the incarcerated person of color. One example of an assumption gleaned from the high incarceration rates of ethnic minorities is that people of color commit more crimes than do European Americans. This research is important in dispelling these types of myths.

The current research can also serve to inform counseling psychology training programs (Morgan et al., 2007). Offenders are ethnically, racially, and culturally diverse, so the need for multicultural training for correctional and forensic psychologists is especially relevant (Morgan, Rozycki, & Wilson, 2004). Part of multicultural training for correctional and forensic psychologists should include exploring the psychologist's perceptions, biases, beliefs, and values toward criminal offenders. The current research can be used to help these psychologists explore their myths, and help them understand the impact of bias and racism on the inmates or parolees of color they work with, and help build more empathy toward this population.

Suggestions for Future Research

This study raised many questions relating to the variables of just world beliefs, attitudes toward the punishment of criminals, and ethnicity and how these interplay and impact juror bias. Future research might want to explore how the relationship of an individual's experience with the criminal justice system, either directly or vicariously, impacts a person's beliefs in a just world. Experience with the justice system might have been a possible confound of the current study and the relationship between these two variables in not well known. Experience with the criminal justice system may also impact a participant's score on the Attitudes Toward the Punishment of Criminals scale. This is also an area that needs more exploration in terms of using this scale to look at juror bias.

Gender role socialization may also have impacted this study. Not much is known regarding how gender impacts Just World Beliefs scores, Attitudes Toward the Punishment of Criminals scores, or how males and females differ in terms of their beliefs toward sentencing. Future studies may need to look at how males and females differ on these scales and either present hypotheses, control for gender, or look at gender as a confounding variable.

In addition, given that this research was concerned with the differences between the ethnicities of Hispanic Americans and European Americans, future research may want to consider using an acculturation scale to ascertain how alike or different Hispanic Americans are to European Americans in culture and worldview. In the current study, both Hispanic Americans and European Americans had nearly identical just world beliefs. It is unknown what role acculturation may have played in this finding.

The Just World Belief scale used in this study by Rubin and Peplau (1975) measures a global belief in a just world and does not consider individual dimensions such as the Furnham and Proctor (1992) Multidimensional Belief in a Just World Scale. This scale might have found different results on some of the dimensions of just world beliefs. In addition, the Rubin and Peplau scale had low reliability with this particular participant sample, which impacted the results.

Future research might also want to explore the impact of socioeconomic status (SES). There is little research that looks at the impact of high versus low SES on the variables explored in this current study. SES may be a variable of interest or one which may need to be controlled. Based upon the literature review one could certainly hypothesize SES would have an impact.

Summary

This study explored the relationships between participant jurors' just world beliefs, attitudes toward the punishment of criminals, juror ethnicity, and ethnicity of the criminal defendant to juror bias, as measured by the Attitudes Toward the Punishment of Criminals Scale and Juror sentencing decisions. The general research questions pursued were (1) does the ethnicity of the juror affect his or her decisions when the criminal defendant is of the same, or of a different ethnicity, than the juror, (2) Is there a difference between ethnicities regarding beliefs that the world is just, (3) Is there a difference between ethnicities regarding attitudes toward the punishment of criminals, and (4) Does a juror's belief regarding the world as a just place affect his or her decision-making regarding a criminal defendant? Seven hypotheses were presented, and none were found significant.

In the current study, there were no differences between Hispanic Americans and European Americans in their just world beliefs, attitudes toward the punishment of criminals, or sentencing decisions toward a criminal defendant. Just world beliefs were not correlated to a juror's attitudes toward the punishment of criminals or sentence length. Nor were juror's attitudes toward the punishment of criminals correlated to sentence length.

The model hypothesized to predict juror bias was not found to be significant statistically, but approached significance at p = .053, r2 = .10. Had the model predicted been significant, the variables of the juror's just world beliefs, random assignment of the ethnicity of the criminal defendant, and the ethnicity of the juror would have predicted 10% of the variance found in participants' Attitudes Toward the Punishment of Criminals scores, which was used to measure juror bias for this hypothesis. Just world beliefs as a significant predictor of juror bias as measured by the Attitudes Toward the Punishment of Criminals Scale was not found significant.

However one interesting discovery resulted from the analysis conducted on hypothesis four. The random assignment of the ethnicity of the criminal defendant as a predictor of juror bias as measured by the ATPC scale was salient p = .01. This is an interesting, but predictable finding, and supports other research regarding ethnicity of the defendant being related to judgments of guilt and sentence length (Abwender and Hough, 2001; Dane and Wrightsman, 1982; Ugwuegbu, 1979; Wuensch et al., 2002). In the current study, more bias was held toward European American criminal defendants than either the African American or Hispanic American criminal defendants. This contradicts the current criminals justice statistics and other research, which demonstrate that Hispanic Americans and African Americans have overall longer incarceration rates than do European Americans (Bureau of Justice Statistics, 2006; Criminal Offender Statistics, 2006; Facts About Prisoners and Prisons, 2007). For this study, participant bias toward European American defendants did not significantly impact their sentencing decisions toward a criminal defendant. However while this is an interesting finding, since the entire predicted model was not significant, no conclusions can be reached from this result. More exploration of this discovery is necessary with additional research.

In addition, future research might explore the impact of the relationship of an individual's experience with the criminal justice system, either directly or vicariously impacts a person's beliefs in a just world and attitudes toward the punishment of criminals. In addition, acculturation and gender socialization may also play a role in a participant's just world beliefs and attitudes that may impact juror bias.

Appendix A
Online Informed Consent

You were chosen as a participant in this study because you could someday be a potential juror in a criminal case. The purpose of this study is to investigate the relationship of ethnicity and just world beliefs on juror decisions toward criminal defendant sentencing. You will be asked to fill out the following instruments: Attitudes Toward the Punishment of Criminals Scale and the Just World Beliefs Scale. You will also be asked to fill out a demographic sheet and read a case vignette in which information is given to you in regard to a simulated criminal case. The actual picture you will see on the arrest card is not the actual person arrested for this crime. The picture is there to simulate an actual arrest card. After reading this case you will be asked to play the role of a juror and decide on a sentence for the crime for which the defendant was found guilty.

There are no known physical, social, legal, spiritual, or economic risks associated with this research. However, there may be a risk of uncomfortable feelings associated with answering these questions. If you have any concerns regarding these questions or this process, please inform the researcher. Also, as a student at the university you have access to counseling at the NMSU counseling center at Garcia Annex. You may call them at 646-2731 if you would like to explore personal issues relating to involvement in this research.

Involvement in this study enables you to contribute to the knowledge base regarding the relationship of ethnicity and just world beliefs on juror decisions of sentencing. Some of you may be involved in classes that offer extra credit for participating in this research.

As a participant in this study, your confidentiality will be maintained. The study asks for no information that would singularly identify you. All data and information gathered from this study will be reflected in total group statistics. You will need to provide your e-mail address, which will only be used as a means for notifying your professor that you are eligible to receive extra credit for participating in a study.

Your participation in this study should encompass no more than 30-45 minutes on one occasion. If you have any questions regarding your rights as a research participant you may call to get information on how to contact a representative of the Institutional Review Board (IRB) at 646-7177. If you have any questions regarding the research or wish to be informed as to the results of this study, you may contact Melinda Haley at melinda@nmsu.edu or 646-2121.

I understand that I may withdraw at any time from participation in this study without consequence. By clicking the "Next" link below I am indicating my consent to participate in this research project and that I understand the information presented on this informed consent.

Appendix B
Demographics

Please read the following questions and circle the choice that best represents you. For each question only choose _one_ answer. For example, if you are of mixed heritage please choose the ethnicity that you most identify with culturally. For those answers you *write* in, please print and write clearly.

1. I am 1 = Male
   2 = Female

2. My age is ______________.

3. The primary ethnicity I identify with is: 1 = European American
   2 = Hispanic American
   3 = other __________.

4. What is the highest level of education achieved by your father?

   1 = Some grade school
   2 = Some high school but did not graduate
   3 = Graduated from high school
   4 = Some college but did not graduate
   5 = Graduated from college with a bachelor's degree
   6 = Graduated from college with a Master's degree
   7 = Graduated from college with a Doctoral degree (e.g. Ph.D., M.D., Ed.D.).

5. What is the highest level of education achieved by your mother?

   1 = Some grade school
   2 = Some high school but did not graduate
   3 = Graduated from high school

4 = Some college but did not graduate

5 = Graduated from college with a bachelor's degree

6 = Graduated from college with a Master's degree

7 = Graduated from college with a Doctoral degree (e.g. Ph.D., M.D., Ed.D.).

6. What is/was your father's primary job?

7. What is/was our mother's primary job?

Appendix C

European American Case Vignette

Arrest Card—Working Copy

14-JUN-05 9:50

Booking # 501502260767 **Booking Date:** 6/13/05 **Booking Time:** 1:53 pm **PIN:** 0221038311

Arresting Agency ID: LC0589630 **Agency Offence #:** 501502260842 **OSTS:** 9712028259

Name: Christianson, Daniel **DOB:** June 18, 1980

POB: LC **Sex:** Male **Hgt:** 5'11" **Hair:** Brown

Race: Caucasian **Wgt:** 150 **Eyes:** Blue

Residence: 2200 Corley Drive

City: Las Cruces **State:** NM **ZIP:** 88001

Misc ID:
Scars/marks:

Chg.	Statute	Charge Description	Class	Bond	Type	Argn. Date	Docket
1	30-16-3	BURGLARY	F	5000.00	AB	07/16/05	

Disposition: t#: **Disp: CIRCUIT COURT RETURN**

Arrest Date: 6/13/05 **Arrest Time:** 1:53 pm **Arrest Location:** 504 E. Picacho Ave.

Arresting Officer: Aaro, Patrick **ID:** 1510 **Agency Info:** SSO#07-4256

Employed by: APAC Construction **Occupation:** Construction Laborer **Emp Phone:**

Release Date: **Release Time:**

Defendant Biography

Daniel Christianson is a Caucasian male, age 25, who has worked in the field of construction since he dropped out of high school at age 16. Daniel initially dropped out of school to help support his family when his father was laid off from his job. Daniel has not returned to school, although he would like to some day. Daniel's family has lived in Las Cruces since Daniel was three years old. Daniel, the oldest sibling in the family, has three brothers and one sister who all still live at home. Daniel lives in a small apartment over the family's garage.

Daniel has worked at a variety of construction jobs as a contract laborer, and has garnered a variety of skills and experiences. However, as his employment is seasonal, Daniel has often found it difficult to make ends meet. Daniel has been employed by a local contractor, APAC Construction, at the same job site for the last six months. This is the most time he has spent working on one job, for one contractor. Over the past two years Daniel has been employed as a contract laborer for six different construction firms. The longest period of time he has not worked was four months. Daniel often fills in during the off season with jobs at local restaurants to help pay his bills.

Daniel is single and has never been married, but he has been in a long term relationship with his girlfriend for the past 18 months. Daniel was planning on asking his girlfriend to marry him next Valentine's day. Daniel's pride and joy is his blue 1991 Ford, F150, short-bed pickup truck. Daniel is proud of his truck because he fixed it up himself and has added personal touches such as red flames on the rear quarter panels, a chrome roll bar, and a Snoopy decal on the window, which has been his trademark since high school.

Daniel is currently charged with felony burglary and is being held in the Las Cruces detention center awaiting trial. He has been in the detention center for the last two months because he has not been able to post the $5000.00 bond. Daniel has no prior criminal record, or history of trouble with the law.

Arresting Officer's Report

1a. From: (Name of arresting officer- Last, First, MI) Delgado, Jacob, T.	b. Department/Precinct Las Cruces Police Dept/ 003	c. DATE OF REPORT June 13, 2005
2a. Report Number LC562841-F	b. Charge/Statute/Description/Class 1 30-16-3 Felony Burglary	
3a. NAME OF ACCUSED (Last, First, MI) Christianson, Daniel	b. SSN 544-92-3017	c. DATE OF CHARGES 7/16/05

4a. Date of Birth	b. Height	c. Weight	c. Hair color	d. Eye Color
June 18, 1980	5'11"	150 lbs	Brown	Blue

(Check appropriate answer)	YES	NO
4. In accordance with Las Cruces Police Department regulations, I have investigated the charges Appended hereto (Exhibit 1)	X	
5. At the beginning of the investigation I informed the accused of: (***check appropriate answer)***	YES	NO
a. The charges(s) under investigation	X	
b. The identity of the accuser	X	
c. The right against self-incrimination	X	
d. The purpose of the investigation	X	
e. The right to be present throughout the taking of evidence.	X	
f. The right to make a sworn, or unsworn statement, orally or in writing.	X	

6. State the circumstances and describe the proceedings conducted in the investigation.

At 0930 hours on 13 June 05, dispatch received a call from Mr. George Gerber of 1420 E. Picacho Ave., regarding missing tools from his residence. Mr. Gerber, the homeowner stated his 11-year-old son accidentally left the garage door open when removing his bike to go to school the previous morning. Homeowner did not notice the tools missing until 0900 this morning. Upon request, Mr. Gerber was able to provide a written list of tool manufacture names, tool brands, and serial numbers he had listed under his homeowner's insurance policy. Mr. Gerber verified these were the missing tools.

Witnesses (Jim Baker at 1421 E. Picacho Ave) and (Melody Kincaid at 1419 E. Picacho Ave) stated they saw a blue, Ford F150, short bed pickup truck with a chrome roll bar, and a snoopy decal, parked in front of the residence yesterday morning around 1100 hours. The truck had red flames painted on the rear quarter panel. Neither witness got the license plate number of the vehicle, nor saw anyone in or around Mr. Gerber's garage. Homeowner and witnesses said the vehicle is frequently seen in the area, but does not live on this street.

After driving around the neighborhood, a vehicle matching the description provided by the witnesses was spotted at an APAC construction site. Upon inspecting the vehicle from the outside, tools matching the description of the homeowner were clearly visible inside the cab of the truck. The driver of the vehicle was identified and he voluntarily allowed officer to inspect the tools. The manufacture, tool brand, and serial numbers on the tools matched those described by Mr. Gerber. Daniel Christianson was read his rights and was arrested without incident. Suspect claimed he bought the tools that morning, but would not provide a description of the male who sold the tools to him.

Note: If additional space is required for any item, enter the additional material on a separate sheet. Identify such material with the proper numerical and, if appropriate, lettered heading (Example "1C"). Securely attach any additional sheets to the form and add a note in the appropriate item of the form: "See additional sheet."

DD Form 457, AUG 84 (EG) EDITION OF OCT 69 IS OBSOLETE. Designed by WHS/DIOR, Oct, 84

Investigating Officer's Report

Page 1 of 2

1a. From: (Name of Investigating officer- Last, First, MI)	b. Department/Precinct	c. DATE OF REPORT
Yurbo, David A.	Las Cruces Police Dept/ 003	June 17, 2005

2a. Arrest Report Number	b. Charge/Statute/Description/Class
LC562841-F	1 30-16-3 Felony Burglary

3a. NAME OF ACCUSED (Last, First, MI)	b. SSN	c. DATE OF CHARGES
Christianson, Daniel	544-92-3017	7/16/05

4a. Date of Birth	b. Height	c. Weight	c. Hair color	d. Eye Color
June 18, 1980	5'11"	150 lbs	Brown	Blue

5. Witnesses Interviewed	Telephone or Address	Method of Interview
a. Jim Baker	1421 E. Picacho Ave, Las Cruces	In-Person
b. Melody Kincaid	1419 E. Picacho Ave. Las Cruces	In-Person
c. Jesus Caballo	520 Walnut street, Las Cruces	In-Person
d. Jonathan Castillo	2232 Lohman Ave, Las Cruces	In-Person
e.		

Note: If additional space is required for any item, enter the additional material on a separate sheet. Identify such material with the proper numerical and, if appropriate, lettered heading (Example "1C"). Securely attach any additional sheets to the form and add a note in the appropriate item of the form: "See additional sheet."

Witness Statements

5a. I saw a blue Ford truck, F150, short bed parked in front of the residence from about 11:00am to maybe 11:15 am or so. It had red flames on the rear quarter panel and a chrome roll bar. I've seen this truck going down this street quite a bit, but I don't think he (the driver) lives on the street. I haven't seen the truck parked in front of any house around here so I really don't think the person lives in this neighborhood. I did not see anyone in the truck, nor did I see anyone in the garage. I did not get the license plate number either.

5b. I saw a blue truck parked out in front of the house. It was really distinctive as it had red flames on the back and a snoopy decal in the window. I'm not sure what kind of truck it was, but it was older, and it was fixed up nice. It had a roll bar in back too. I did not see who was driving it, but I've seen it drive down this street before and it is driven by a Caucasian man.

5c. I saw Daniel arrive at the job site at about 8:15 this morning. I saw him talking to a man who approached him. They talked for about 2 minutes, and then Daniel walked over to the crew boss, got his assignment for the day, and began to work. I did not see where the other man went, but he was not a part of our crew. The man did not appear to have anything in his hands when talking to Daniel. I did not see anything change hands between them. I did not see Daniel talking to the man again that day.

5d. I am Daniel Christianson's employer. I told Daniel two months ago that he needed to purchase his own power tools for this job site, or else I would have to let him go. I told him last week that if he did not have the tools by June 30th, I would have to fire him. I did not see anything unusual on the day you are asking about. I did not see Daniel talking to anyone other than my crew.

5e.

Investigating Officer's Report

Note: If additional space is required for any item, enter the additional material on a separate sheet. Identify such material with the proper numerical and, if appropriate, lettered heading (Example "1C"). Securely attach any additional sheets to the form and add a note in the appropriate item of the form: "See additional sheet."

6. **Suspect Statement**: When I arrived at the job site a man approached me and told me he was down on his luck and needed to sell some tools. He told me what tools they were, and they were tools I needed for work here at this job site. The man showed me the tools that were in his car. I asked him how much they were and he told me $300.00. I told the man if he came back later, I would pay him for the tools. I called my girlfriend and asked her to bring me the money, and she did. When the man came back about 30 minutes later with the tools, I bought them. I drive through the neighborhood everyday on my way to work. I stopped on the street yesterday to pick up a lit cigarette that fell onto the floorboard of my truck. I was trying to get the burn mark off my floor mat.

7. **Investigating Officer Remarks**

The tools collected from the suspect's truck had Daniel Christianson's fingerprints on them. The tools also had Mr. Gerber (the homeowner's) fingerprints on them, but no additional fingerprints were found on any of the tools. Mr. Christianson refused to give a physical description of the man he states sold him the tools. Witnesses place Mr. Christianson's truck in front of the residence of Mr. Gerber the day the garage door was left open. No one saw any one in, or around, the garage of Mr. Gerber on the day in question. Daniel Christianson was cooperative with this investigation, except for his refusal to give a description of the man in question that had sold him the tools.

8. **Physical Evidence**

Heavy Duty Random Orbit Palm Sander - DeWalt (DW420), Serial Number: 52A61D, value $118.80
Drywall Screwdriver (Variable Speed, Reversible) - Makita (6821); Serial Number: MK629564, value $129.60
7-1/4" Electric Circular Saw Skil#5150-46, Serial Number: DPO9812-8-45-2, value $75.60
1-1/8" Electric Rotary Hammer, Milwaukee #5303-80, Serial Number: 255KLP6485, value $645.84
Total value of items: 969.84

9. Investigating Officer's Signature	10. Date June 2005

PREVIOUS EDITIONS OF THIS FORM ARE OBSOLETE Form 972, SEPT 2000

Office of the District ATTORNEY—18th JUDICIAL DISTRICT

VICTIM STATEMENT

Note the * indicates a required field.
Defendants/Offenders Name:

* First	Daniel
Middle	
* Last	Christianson
*Case Number	**50150226084**

IF YOU DO NOT WISH TO MAKE A STATEMENT: PLEASE CHECK THIS BOX ☐ AND ENTER YOUR NAME AT THE BOTTOM OF THIS PAGE.

As a victim of a crime, we want to give you the chance to share your feelings about how this crime has affected you. While we realize it may be hard to put in writing, we feel it is important to have your thoughts. State in your own words how this crime has affected you and/or your family. This information will be kept in the official case file and will be made available during the pre-sentence investigation and to the judge before sentencing of the defendant/offender (if convicted).

> My family and I feel violated! My eleven-year-old son is inconsolable, as it is he who left the garage door open. These tools took years for me to acquire, and because of one mistake, they are gone. We are not rich, and I cannot replace these tools. I don't know what else to say, except I feel really violated, cheated, and victimized.

* Your Name: George Gerber

Entering your name in the above field and clicking the submit button below constitutes your electronic signature of this form.

Appendix D

Hispanic American Case Vignette

Arrest Card—Working Copy

14-JUN-05 9:50

Booking # 501502260767 **Booking Date:** 6/13/05 **Booking Time:** 1:53 pm **PIN:** 0221038311

Arresting Agency ID: LC0589630 **Agency Offence #:** 501502260842 **OSTS:** 9712028259

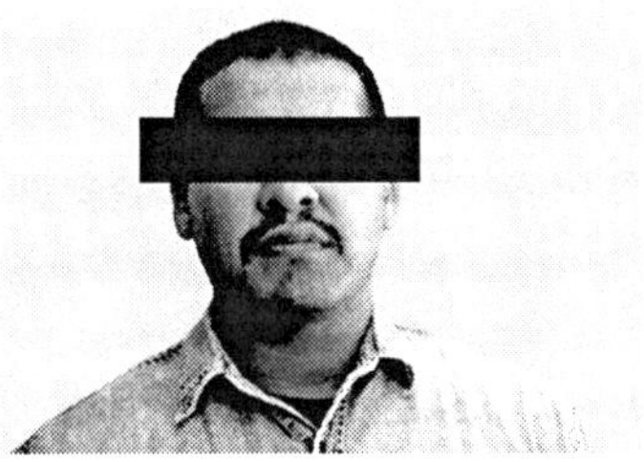

Name: Rodríguez, Hector **DOB:** June 18, 1980

POB: LC **Sex:** Male **Hgt:** 5'11" **Hair:** Brown

Race: Hispanic **Wgt:** 150 **Eyes:** Brown

Residence: 2200 Corley Drive

City: Las Cruces **State:** NM **ZIP:** 88001

Misc ID:
Scars/marks:

Chg.	Statute	Charge Description	Class	Bond	Type	Argn. Date	Docket
1	30-16-3	BURGLARY	F	5000.00	AB	07/16/05	

Disposition: t#: **Disp: CIRCUIT COURT RETURN**

Arrest Date: 6/13/05 **Arrest Time:** 1:53 pm **Arrest Location:** 504 E. Picacho Ave.

Arresting Officer: Aaro, Patrick **ID:** 1510 **Agency Info:** SSO#07-4256

Employed by: APAC Construction **Occupation:** Construction Laborer **Emp Phone:**

Release Date: **Release Time:**

Defendant Biography

Hector Rodriguez is a Hispanic male, age 25, who has worked in the field of construction since he dropped out of high school at age 16. Hector initially dropped out of school to help support his family when his father was laid off from his job. Hector has not returned to school, although he would like to some day. Hector's family has lived in Las Cruces since Hector was three years old. Hector, the oldest sibling in the family, has three brothers and one sister who all still live at home. Hector lives in a small apartment over the family's garage.

Hector has worked at a variety of construction jobs as a contract laborer, and has garnered a variety of skills and experiences. However, as his employment is seasonal, Hector has often found it difficult to make ends meet. Hector has been employed by a local contractor, APAC Construction, at the same job site for the last six months. This is the most time he has spent working on one job, for one contractor. Over the past two years Hector has been employed as a contract laborer for six different construction firms. The longest period of time he has not worked was four months. Hector often fills in during the off season with jobs at local restaurants to help pay his bills.

Hector is single and has never been married, but he has been in a long term relationship with his girlfriend for the past 18 months. Hector was planning on asking his girlfriend to marry him next Valentine's day. Hector's pride and joy is his blue 1991 Ford, F150, short-bed pickup truck. Hector is proud of his truck because he fixed it up himself and has added personal touches such as red flames on the rear quarter panels, a chrome roll bar, and a Snoopy decal on the window, which has been his trademark since high school.

Hector is currently charged with felony burglary and is being held in the Las Cruces detention center awaiting trial. He has been in the detention center for the last two months because he has not been able to post the $5000.00 bond. Hector has no prior criminal record, or history of trouble with the law.

Arresting Officer's Report

1a. From: (Name of arresting officer- Last, First, MI) Delgado, Jacob, T.	b. Department/Precinct Las Cruces Police Dept/ 003	c. DATE OF REPORT June 13, 2005
2a. Report Number LC562841-F	b. Charge/Statute/Description/Class 1 30-16-3 Felony Burglary	
3a. NAME OF ACCUSED (Last, First, MI) Rodriguez, Hector	b. SSN 544-92-3017	c. DATE OF CHARGES 7/16/05

4a. Date of Birth	b. Height	c. Weight	c. Hair color	d. Eye Color
June 18, 1980	5'11"	150 lbs	Brown	Brown

(Check appropriate answer)	YES	NO
4. In accordance with Las Cruces Police Department regulations, I have investigated the charges Appended hereto (Exhibit 1)	X	
5. At the beginning of the investigation I informed the accused of: (***check appropriate answer)***	YES	NO
a. The charges(s) under investigation	X	
b. The identity of the accuser	X	
c. The right against self-incrimination	X	
d. The purpose of the investigation	X	
e. The right to be present throughout the taking of evidence.	X	
f. The right to make a sworn, or unsworn statement, orally or in writing.	X	

6. State the circumstances and describe the proceedings conducted in the investigation.

At 0930 hours on 13 June 05, dispatch received a call from Mr. George Gerber of 1420 E. Picacho Ave., regarding missing tools from his residence. Mr. Gerber, the homeowner stated his 11-year-old son accidentally left the garage door open when removing his bike to go to school the previous morning. Homeowner did not notice the tools missing until 0900 this morning. Upon request, Mr. Gerber was able to provide a written list of tool manufacture names, tool brands, and serial numbers he had listed under his homeowner's insurance policy. Mr. Gerber verified these were the missing tools.

Witnesses (Jim Baker at 1421 E. Picacho Ave) and (Melody Kincaid at 1419 E. Picacho Ave) stated they saw a blue, Ford F150, short bed pickup truck with a chrome roll bar, and a snoopy decal, parked in front of the residence yesterday morning around 1100 hours. The truck had red flames painted on the rear quarter panel. Neither witness got the license plate number of the vehicle, nor saw anyone in or around Mr. Gerber's garage. Homeowner and witnesses said the vehicle is frequently seen in the area, but does not live on this street.

After driving around the neighborhood, a vehicle matching the description provided by the witnesses was spotted at an APAC construction site. Upon inspecting the vehicle from the outside, tools matching the description of the homeowner were clearly visible inside the cab of the truck. The driver of the vehicle was identified and he voluntarily allowed officer to inspect the tools. The manufacture, tool brand, and serial numbers on the tools matched those described by Mr. Gerber. Hector Rodriguez was read his rights and was arrested without incident. Suspect claimed he bought the tools that morning, but would not provide a description of the male who sold the tools to him.

Note: If additional space is required for any item, enter the additional material on a separate sheet. Identify such material with the proper numerical and, if appropriate, lettered heading (Example "1C"). Securely attach any additional sheets to the form and add a note in the appropriate item of the form: "See additional sheet."

DD Form 457, AUG 84 (EG) EDITION OF OCT 69 IS OBSOLETE. Designed by WHS/DIOR, Oct 84

Investigating Officer's Report

Page 1 of 2

1a. From: (Name of Investigating officer- Last, First, MI)	b. Department/Precinct	c. DATE OF REPORT
Yurbo, David A.	Las Cruces Police Dept/ 003	June 17, 2005

2a. Arrest Report Number	b. Charge/Statute/Description/Class
LC562841-F	1 30-16-3 Felony Burglary

3a. NAME OF ACCUSED (Last, First, MI)	b. SSN	c. DATE OF CHARGES
Rodriguez, Hector	544-92-3017	7/16/05

4a. Date of Birth	b. Height	c. Weight	c. Hair color	d. Eye Color
June 18, 1980	5'11"	150 lbs	Brown	Brown

5. Witnesses Interviewed	Telephone or Address	Method of Interview
a. Jim Baker	1421 E. Picacho Ave, Las Cruces	In-Person
b. Melody Kincaid	1419 E. Picacho Ave. Las Cruces	In-Person
c. Jesus Caballo	520 Walnut street, Las Cruces	In-Person
d. Jonathan Castillo	2232 Lohman Ave, Las Cruces	In-Person
e.		

Note: If additional space is required for any item, enter the additional material on a separate sheet. Identify such material with the proper numerical and, if appropriate, lettered heading (Example "1C"). Securely attach any additional sheets to the form and add a note in the appropriate item of the form: "See additional sheet."

Witness Statements

5a. I saw a blue Ford truck, F150, short bed parked in front of the residence from about 11:00am to maybe 11:15 am or so. It had red flames on the rear quarter panel and a chrome roll bar. I've seen this truck going down this street quite a bit, but I don't think he (the driver) lives on the street. I haven't seen the truck parked in front of any house around here so I really don't think the person lives in this neighborhood. I did not see anyone in the truck, nor did I see anyone in the garage. I did not get the license plate number either.

5b. I saw a blue truck parked out in front of the house. It was really distinctive as it had red flames on the back and a snoopy decal in the window. I'm not sure what kind of truck it was, but it was older, and it was fixed up nice. It had a roll bar in back too. I did not see who was driving it, but I've seen it drive down this street before and it is driven by a Hispanic man.

5c. I saw Hector arrive at the job site at about 8:15 this morning. I saw him talking to a man who approached him. They talked for about 2 minutes, and then Hector walked over to the crew boss, got his assignment for the day, and began to work. I did not see where the other man went, but he was not a part of our crew. The man did not appear to have anything in his hands when talking to Hector. I did not see anything change hands between them. I did not see Hector talking to the man again that day.

5d. I am Hector Rodriguez's employer. I told Hector two months ago that he needed to purchase his own power tools for this job site, or else I would have to let him go. I told him last week that if he did not have the tools by June 30th, I would have to fire him. I did not see anything unusual on the day you are asking about. I did not see Hector talking to anyone other than my crew.

5e.

Investigating Officer's Report
Page 2 of 2

Note: If additional space is required for any item, enter the additional material on a separate sheet. Identify such material with the proper numerical and, if appropriate, lettered heading (Example "1C"). Securely attach any additional sheets to the form and add a note in the appropriate item of the form: "See additional sheet."

6. **Suspect Statement**: When I arrived at the job site a man approached me and told me he was down on his luck and needed to sell some tools. He told me what tools they were, and they were tools I needed for work here at this job site. The man showed me the tools that were in his car. I asked him how much they were and he told me $300.00. I told the man if he came back later, I would pay him for the tools. I called my girlfriend and asked her to bring me the money, and she did. When the man came back about 30 minutes later with the tools, I bought them. I drive through the neighborhood everyday on my way to work. I stopped on the street yesterday to pick up a lit cigarette that fell onto the floorboard of my truck. I was trying to get the burn mark off my floor mat.

7. **Investigating Officer Remarks**
The tools collected from the suspect's truck had Hector Rodriguez's fingerprints on them. The tools also had Mr. Gerber (the homeowner's) fingerprints on them, but no additional fingerprints were found on any of the tools. Mr. Rodriguez refused to give a physical description of the man he states sold him the tools. Witnesses place Mr. Rodriguez's truck in front of the residence of Mr. Gerber the day the garage door was left open. No one saw any one in, or around, the garage of Mr. Gerber on the day in question. Hector Rodriguez was cooperative with this investigation, except for his refusal to give a description of the man in question that had sold him the tools.

8. **Physical Evidence**
Heavy Duty Random Orbit Palm Sander - DeWalt (DW420), Serial Number: 52A61D, value $118.80
Drywall Screwdriver (Variable Speed, Reversible) - Makita (6821); Serial Number: MK629564, value $129.60
7-1/4" Electric Circular Saw Skil#5150-46, Serial Number: DPO9812-8-45-2, value $75.60
1-1/8" Electric Rotary Hammer, Milwaukee #5303-80, Serial Number: 255KLP6485, value $645.84
Total value of items: 969.84

9. Investigating Officer's Signature	10. Date June 2005

PREVIOUS EDITIONS OF THIS FORM ARE OBSOLETE Form 972, SEPT 2000

Office of the District ATTORNEY—18th JUDICIAL DISTRICT

VICTIM STATEMENT

Note the * indicates a required field.
Defendants/Offenders Name:

* First	Hector
Middle	
* Last	Rodriguez
*Case Number	**50150226084**

IF YOU DO NOT WISH TO MAKE A STATEMENT: PLEASE CHECK THIS BOX ☐ND ENTER YOUR NAME AT THE BOTTOM OF THIS PAGE.

As a victim of a crime, we want to give you the chance to share your feelings about how this crime has affected you. While we realize it may be hard to put in writing, we feel it is important to have your thoughts. State in your own words how this crime has affected you and/or your family. This information will be kept in the official case file and will be made available during the pre-sentence investigation and to the judge before sentencing of the defendant/offender (if convicted).

My family and I feel violated! My eleven-year-old son is inconsolable, as it is he who left the garage door open. These tools took years for me to acquire, and because of one mistake, they are gone. We are not rich, and I cannot replace these tools. I don't know what else to say, except I feel really violated, cheated, and victimized.

* Your Name | George Gerber

Entering your name in the above field and clicking the submit button below constitutes your electronic signature of this form.

Appendix E
African American Case Vignette

Arrest Card—Working Copy

14-JUN-05 9:50

Booking # 501502260767 **Booking Date:** 6/13/05 **Booking Time:** 1:53 pm **PIN:** 0221038311

Arresting Agency ID: LC0589630 **Agency Offence #:** 501502260842 **OSTS:** 9712028259

Name: Washington, Jerome **DOB:** June 18, 1980

POB: LC **Sex:** Male **Hgt:** 5'11" **Hair:** Black

Race: Black **Wgt:** 150 **Eyes:** Brown

Residence: 2200 Corley Drive

City: Las Cruces **State:** NM **ZIP:** 88001

Misc ID:
Scars/marks:

Chg.	Statute	Charge Description	Class	Bond	Type	Argn. Date	Docket
1	30-16-3	BURGLARY	F	5000.00	AB	07/16/05	

Disposition: t#: **Disp: CIRCUIT COURT RETURN**

Arrest Date: 6/13/05 **Arrest Time:** 1:53 pm **Arrest Location:** 504 E. Picacho Ave.

Arresting Officer: Aaro, Patrick **ID:** 1510 **Agency Info:** SSO#07-4256

Employed by: APAC Construction **Occupation:** Construction Laborer **Emp Phone:**

Release Date: **Release Time:**

Defendant Biography

Jerome Washington is a Black male, age 25, who has worked in the field of construction since he dropped out of high school at age 16. Jerome initially dropped out of school to help support his family when his father was laid off from his job. Jerome has not returned to school, although he would like to some day. Jerome's family has lived in Las Cruces since Jerome was three years old. Jerome, the oldest sibling in the family, has three brothers and one sister who all still live at home. Jerome lives in a small apartment over the family's garage.

Jerome has worked at a variety of construction jobs as a contract laborer, and has garnered a variety of skills and experiences. However, as his employment is seasonal, Jerome has often found it difficult to make ends meet. Jerome has been employed by a local contractor, APAC Construction, at the same job site for the last six months. This is the most time he has spent working on one job, for one contractor. Over the past two years Jerome has been employed as a contract laborer for six different construction firms. The longest period of time he has not worked was four months. Jerome often fills in during the off season with jobs at local restaurants to help pay his bills.

Jerome is single and has never been married, but he has been in a long term relationship with his girlfriend for the past 18 months. Jerome was planning on asking his girlfriend to marry him next Valentine's day. Jerome's pride and joy is his blue 1991 Ford, F150, short-bed pickup truck. Jerome is proud of his truck because he fixed it up himself and has added personal touches such as red flames on the rear quarter panels, a chrome roll bar, and a Snoopy decal on the window, which has been his trademark since high school.

Jerome is currently charged with felony burglary and is being held in the Las Cruces detention center awaiting trial. He has been in the detention center for the last two months because he has not been able to post the $5000.00 bond. Jerome has no prior criminal record, or history of trouble with the law.

Arresting Officer's Report

1a. From: (Name of arresting officer- Last, First, MI)	b. Department/Precinct	c. DATE OF REPORT
Delgado, Jacob, T.	Las Cruces Police Dept/ 003	June 13, 2005

2a. Report Number	b. Charge/Statute/Description/Class
LC562841-F	1 30-16-3 Felony Burglary

3a. NAME OF ACCUSED (Last, First, MI)	b. SSN	c. DATE OF CHARGES
Washington, Jerome	544-92-3017	7/16/05

4a. Date of Birth	b. Height	c. Weight	c. Hair color	d. Eye Color
June 18, 1980	5'11"	150 lbs	Black	Brown

(Check appropriate answer)	YES	NO
4. In accordance with Las Cruces Police Department regulations, I have investigated the charges Appended hereto (Exhibit 1)	X	
5. At the beginning of the investigation I informed the accused of: (***check appropriate answer)***	YES	NO
a. The charges(s) under investigation	X	
b. The identity of the accuser	X	
c. The right against self-incrimination	X	
d. The purpose of the investigation	X	
e. The right to be present throughout the taking of evidence.	X	
f. The right to make a sworn, or unsworn statement, orally or in writing.	X	

6. State the circumstances and describe the proceedings conducted in the investigation.

At 0930 hours on 13 June 05, dispatch received a call from Mr. George Gerber of 1420 E. Picacho Ave., regarding missing tools from his residence. Mr. Gerber, the homeowner stated his 11-year-old son accidentally left the garage door open when removing his bike to go to school the previous morning. Homeowner did not notice the tools missing until 0900 this morning. Upon request, Mr. Gerber was able to provide a written list of tool manufacture names, tool brands, and serial numbers he had listed under his homeowner's insurance policy. Mr. Gerber verified these were the missing tools.

Witnesses (Jim Baker at 1421 E. Picacho Ave) and (Melody Kincaid at 1419 E. Picacho Ave) stated they saw a blue, Ford F150, short bed pickup truck with a chrome roll bar, and a snoopy decal, parked in front of the residence yesterday morning around 1100 hours. The truck had red flames painted on the rear quarter panel. Neither witness got the license plate number of the vehicle, nor saw anyone in or around Mr. Gerber's garage. Homeowner and witnesses said the vehicle is frequently seen in the area, but does not live on this street.

After driving around the neighborhood, a vehicle matching the description provided by the witnesses was spotted at an APAC construction site. Upon inspecting the vehicle from the outside, tools matching the description of the homeowner were clearly visible inside the cab of the truck. The driver of the vehicle was identified and he voluntarily allowed officer to inspect the tools. The manufacture, tool brand, and serial numbers on the tools matched those described by Mr. Gerber. Jerome Washington was read his rights and was arrested without incident. Suspect claimed he bought the tools that morning, but would not provide a description of the male who sold the tools to him.

Note: If additional space is required for any item, enter the additional material on a separate sheet. Identify such material with the proper numerical and, if appropriate, lettered heading (Example "1C"). Securely attach any additional sheets to the form and add a note in the appropriate item of the form: "See additional sheet."

DD Form 457, AUG 84 (EG) EDITION OF OCT 69 IS OBSOLETE. Designed by WHS/DIOR, Oct 84

Investigating Officer's Report Page 1 of 2					
1a. From: (Name of Investigating officer- Last, First, MI) Yurbo, David A.	b. Department/Precinct Las Cruces Police Dept/ 003		c. DATE OF REPORT June 17, 2005		
2a. Arrest Report Number LC562841-F	b. Charge/Statute/Description/Class 1 30-16-3 Felony Burglary				
3a. NAME OF ACCUSED (Last, First, MI) Washington, Jerome	b. SSN 544-92-3017		c. DATE OF CHARGES 7/16/05		
4a. Date of Birth June 18, 1980	b. Height 5'11"	c. Weight 150 lbs	c. Hair color Black	d. Eye Color Brown	

5. Witnesses Interviewed	Telephone or Address	Method of Interview
a. Jim Baker	1421 E. Picacho Ave, Las Cruces	In-Person
b. Melody Kincaid	1419 E. Picacho Ave. Las Cruces	In-Person
c. Jesus Caballo	520 Walnut street, Las Cruces	In-Person
d. Jonathan Castillo	2232 Lohman Ave, Las Cruces	In-Person
e.		

Note: If additional space is required for any item, enter the additional material on a separate sheet. Identify such material with the proper numerical and, if appropriate, lettered heading (Example "1C"). Securely attach any additional sheets to the form and add a note in the appropriate item of the form: "See additional sheet."

Witness Statements

5a. I saw a blue Ford truck, F150, short bed parked in front of the residence from about 11:00am to maybe 11:15 am or so. It had red flames on the rear quarter panel and a chrome roll bar. I've seen this truck going down this street quite a bit, but I don't think he (the driver) lives on the street. I haven't seen the truck parked in front of any house around here so I really don't think the person lives in this neighborhood. I did not see anyone in the truck, nor did I see anyone in the garage. I did not get the license plate number either.

5b. I saw a blue truck parked out in front of the house. It was really distinctive as it had red flames on the back and a snoopy decal in the window. I'm not sure what kind of truck it was, but it was older, and it was fixed up nice. It had a roll bar in back too. I did not see who was driving it, but I've seen it drive down this street before and it is driven by a Black man.

5c. I saw Jerome arrive at the job site at about 8:15 this morning. I saw him talking to a man who approached him. They talked for about 2 minutes, and then Jerome walked over to the crew boss, got his assignment for the day, and began to work. I did not see where the other man went, but he was not a part of our crew. The man did not appear to have anything in his hands when talking to Hector. I did not see anything change hands between them. I did not see Jerome talking to the man again that day.

5d. I am Jerome Washington's employer. I told Jerome two months ago that he needed to purchase his own power tools for this job site, or else I would have to let him go. I told him last week that if he did not have the tools by June 30th, I would have to fire him. I did not see anything unusual on the day you are asking about. I did not see Jerome talking to anyone other than my crew.

5e.

Investigating Officer's Report Page 2 of 2

Note: If additional space is required for any item, enter the additional material on a separate sheet. Identify such material with the proper numerical and, if appropriate, lettered heading (Example "1C"). Securely attach any additional sheets to the form and add a note in the appropriate item of the form: "See additional sheet."

6. **Suspect Statement**: When I arrived at the job site a man approached me and told me he was down on his luck and needed to sell some tools. He told me what tools they were, and they were tools I needed for work here at this job site. The man showed me the tools that were in his car. I asked him how much they were and he told me $300.00. I told the man if he came back later, I would pay him for the tools. I called my girlfriend and asked her to bring me the money, and she did. When the man came back about 30 minutes later with the tools, I bought them. I drive through the neighborhood everyday on my way to work. I stopped on the street yesterday to pick up a lit cigarette that fell onto the floorboard of my truck. I was trying to get the burn mark off my floor mat.

7. **Investigating Officer Remarks**

The tools collected from the suspect's truck had Jerome Washington's fingerprints on them. The tools also had Mr. Gerber (the homeowner's) fingerprints on them, but no additional fingerprints were found on any of the tools. Mr. Washington refused to give a physical description of the man he states sold him the tools. Witnesses place Mr. Washington's truck in front of the residence of Mr. Gerber the day the garage door was left open. No one saw any one in, or around, the garage of Mr. Gerber on the day in question. Jerome Washington was cooperative with this investigation, except for his refusal to give a description of the man in question that had sold him the tools.

8. **Physical Evidence**

Heavy Duty Random Orbit Palm Sander - DeWalt (DW420), Serial Number: 52A61D, value $118.80
Drywall Screwdriver (Variable Speed, Reversible) - Makita (6821); Serial Number: MK629564, value $129.60
7-1/4" Electric Circular Saw Skil#5150-46, Serial Number: DPO9812-8-45-2, value $75.60
1-1/8" Electric Rotary Hammer, Milwaukee #5303-80, Serial Number: 255KLP6485, value $645.84
Total value of items: 969.84

9. Investigating Officer's Signature	10. Date June 2005

PREVIOUS EDITIONS OF THIS FORM ARE OBSOLETE Form 972, SEPT 2000

Office of the District ATTORNEY—18th JUDICIAL DISTRICT

VICTIM STATEMENT

Note the * indicates a required field.
Defendants/Offenders Name:

* First	Jerome
Middle	
* Last	Washington
*Case Number	**50150226084**

IF YOU DO NOT WISH TO MAKE A STATEMENT: PLEASE CHECK THIS BOX ☐ AND ENTER YOUR NAME AT THE BOTTOM OF THIS PAGE.

As a victim of a crime, we want to give you the chance to share your feelings about how this crime has affected you. While we realize it may be hard to put in writing, we feel it is important to have your thoughts. State in your own words how this crime has affected you and/or your family. This information will be kept in the official case file and will be made available during the pre-sentence investigation and to the judge before sentencing of the defendant/offender (if convicted).

My family and I feel violated! My eleven-year-old son is inconsolable, as it is he who left the garage door open. These tools took years for me to acquire, and because of one mistake, they are gone. We are not rich, and I cannot replace these tools. I don't know what else to say, except I feel really violated, cheated, and victimized.

* Your Name	George Gerber

Entering your name in the above field and clicking the submit button below constitutes your electronic signature of this form.

Appendix F
Juror Decision Record

The following information is to help you make a decision in this case. The defendant in this case was found guilty for the charge of burglary. The description can be found below. The definition is from the New Mexico Criminal and Traffic Law Manual (2004).

30-16-3 **Burglary**

- Any person who, without authorization, enters a dwelling house with intent to commit any felony or theft therein is guilty of a ***third degree felony***.

You are a juror whose job it is to decide the sentence for the defendant in the case you read. The possible sentence for this crime ranges from (probation and no imprisonment) to a sentence of (36 months imprisonment). Please indicate your choice of sentence below by circling the number that corresponds to the number of months you feel is fair and just for this crime. Note choosing zero would indicate you chose probation and no prison time for this defendant, whereas choosing the number 36, would indicate you chose three years (36 months) of prison time for this defendant.

Number Circled Indicates Number of Months In Sentence

0	**1**	**2**	**3**	**4**	**5**	**6**	**7**
8	**9**	**10**	**11**	**12**	**13**	**14**	**15**
16	**17**	**18**	**19**	**20**	**21**	**22**	**23**
24	**25**	**26**	**27**	**28**	**29**	**30**	**31**
32	**33**	**34**	**36**	**36**			

Appendix G
JWB Scale

Directions: the statements listed below describe different opinions regarding justness. There are no right or wrong answers, only opinions. You are asked to express YOUR feelings about each statement by indicating whether you (1) strongly disagree, (2) disagree, (3) slightly disagree, (4) slightly agree, (5) agree, or (6) strongly agree. Please indicate your opinion by writing the number that best describes your personal attitude in the left-hand margin. Please answer ***every*** item.

1	2	3	4	5	6
Strongly Disagree	Disagree	Slightly Disagree	Slightly Agree	Agree	Strongly Agree

___1. I've found that a person rarely deserves the reputation he has

___2. Basically, the world is a just place.

___3. People who get "lucky breaks" have usually earned their good fortune.

___4. Careful drivers are just as likely to get hurt in traffic accidents as careless ones.

___5. It is a common occurrence for a guilty person to get off free in American courts.

___6. Students almost always deserve the grades they receive in school.

___7. Men who keep in shape have little chance of suffering a heart attack.

___8. The political candidate who sticks up for his principles rarely gets elected.

___9. It is rare for an innocent man to be wrongly sent to jail.

___10. In professional sports, many fouls and infractions never get called by the referee.

___11. By and large, people deserve what they get.

___12. When parents punish their children, it is almost always for good reasons.

1	2	3	4	5	6
Strongly Disagree	Disagree	Slightly Disagree	Slightly Agree	Agree	Strongly Agree

___13. Good deeds often go unnoticed and unrewarded.

___14. Although evil men may hold political power for a while, in the general course of history, good wins out.

___15. In almost any business or profession, people who do their job well, rise to the top.

___16. American parents tend to overlook the things most to be admired in their children.

___17. It is often impossible for a person to receive a fair trial in the USA.

___18. People who meet with misfortune have often brought it on themselves.

___19. Crime doesn't pay.

___20. Many people suffer through absolutely no fault of their own.

Appendix H

ATPC Scale

Directions: The statements listed below describe different opinions regarding the punishment of criminals. There are no right or wrong answers, only opinions. You are asked to express YOUR feelings about each statement by indicating whether you agree or disagree with the statement. Try to indicate either agreement or disagreement for each statement. If you simply cannot decide about a statement, you may mark it with a question mark.

✓ **Put a check mark if you agree with the statement**

X **Put an X if you disagree with the statement**

____1. A person should be imprisoned only for serious offenses.

____2. It is wrong for society to make any of its members suffer.

____3. Hard prison life will keep men from committing crime.

____4. Some criminals do not benefit from punishment

____5. Most prisons are schools of crime.

____6. We should not consider the comfort of a prisoner.

____7. A criminal will go straight only when he finds that prison life is hard.

____8. No punishment can reduce crime.

____9. Prison influence is degenerating.

____10. Only habitual criminals should be punished.

____11. We should employ corporal punishment in dealing with all criminals.

____12. I have no opinion about the treatment of crime.

____13. Punishment of criminals is a disgrace to civilized society.

____14. Solitary confinement will make the criminal penitent.

____15. It is advantageous to society to spare certain criminals.

✓ **Put a check mark if you agree with the statement**

✗ **Put an X if you disagree with the statement**

____16. Only humane treatment can cure criminals.

____17. Harsh imprisonment merely embitters a criminal.

____18. No leniency should be shown to convicts.

____19. Many petty offenders become dangerous criminals after a prison term.

____20. Failure to punish the criminal encourages crime.

____21. Only by extreme brutal punishment can we cure the criminal.

____22. The more severely a man is punished, the greater the criminal he becomes.

____23. A criminal should be punished first and then reformed.

____24. One way to deter men from crime is to make them suffer.

____25. Punishment is wasteful of human life.

____26. A bread and water diet in prison will cure the criminal.

____27. Brutal treatment of a criminal makes him more dangerous.

____28. A jail sentence will cure many criminals of further offenses.

____29. Prison inmates should be put in irons.

____30. We should consider the individual in treating crime.

____31. Even the most vicious criminal should not be harmed.

____32. It is fair for society to punish those who offend against it.

____33. Humane treatment inspires the criminal to be good.

____34. Some punishment is necessary in dealing with the criminal.

REFERENCES

Abwender, D. A., & Hough, K. (2001). Interactive effects of characteristics of defendant and mock juror on U.S. participants' judgment and sentencing recommendations. *Journal of Social Psychology, 41* (5), 603-618.

Agnew, R. (1992). Foundation for a general strain theory of crime and delinquency. *Criminology, 30,* 47-87.

Aguirre, A., & Baker, D. V. (1993). Racial prejudice and the death penalty: A research note. *Social Justice, 20,* 150-156.

Allard, P. (2002). Life sentences: Denying welfare benefits to women convicted of drug offenses. The Sentencing Project. Retrieved March 22, 2005 from http://www.sentencingproject.org/pdfs/9088.pdf.

Alozie, N. O., Simon, J., & Merrill, B. D. (2003). Gender and political orientation in childhood. *The Social Science Journal, 40* (1), 1-18.

Alston, R. J., Harley, D., & Lenhoff, K. (1995). Hirschi's social control theory: A sociological perspective on drug abuse among persons with disabilities. *The Journal of Rehabilitation, 61* (4), 31-45.

Alvarez, A., & Bachman, R. D. (1996). American Indians and sentencing disparity: An Arizona test. *Journal of Criminal Justice, 24* (6), 549-562.

Ancis, J. R., & Szymanski, D. M. (2001). Awareness of White privilege among White counselor trainees. *The Counseling Psychologist, 29* (4), 548-569.

Ausdale, D. V. (1997). Social science is not social reality: Race, values and the defense of scientific racism. *Journal of American Ethnic History, 16* (2), 64-68.

Bachman, J. G., Wallace Jr., J. M., O'Malley, P. M., Johnston, L. D., Kurth, C. L., & Neighbors, H. W. (1991). Racial/ethnic differences in smoking, drinking, and illicit drug use among American high school seniors, 1976-89. *The American Journal of Public Health, 81* (3), 372-378.

Baluch, S. P., Pieterse, A. L., & Bolden, M. A. (2004). Counseling psychology and social justice: Houston...we have a problem. *The Counseling Psychologist, 32* (1), 89-98.

Baratz, J. C., & Baratz, S. S. (1969). *The social pathology model: Historical bases for psychology's denial of the existence of Negro culture.* Washington, D.C.: American Psychological Association.

Barkan, E. (1992). *The retreat of scientific racism.* New York: Cambridge University Press.

Beers, C. W. (1908) *A mind that found itself.* London: Longman's, Green, & Co.

Begue, L. (2002). Beliefs in justice and faith in people: Just world, religiosity, and interpersonal trust. *Personality and Individual Differences, 32,* 375-378.

Berndt, T. J. (1997). *Child development,* 2nd ed. Dubuque, IA: Brown & Benchmark.

Benson, E. (2003, July/Aug). Rehabilitate or punish? *Monitor On Psychology, 34* (7), 46.

Bernstein, I. N., Kelly, W. R., & Doyle, P. A. (1977). Societal reaction to deviants: The case of criminal defendants. *American Sociological Review, 42* (5), 743-755.

Blakey, M. L. (1999 Spring-Summer). Scientific racism and the biological concept of race. *Literature and Psychology* 29, 49-62.

Blumer, H. (1958). Race prejudice as a sense of group position. *Pacific Sociological Review 1,* 3-7.

Bobo, L., & Hutchings, V. L. (1996). Perceptions of racial group competition: Extending Blumer's theory group position to a multiracial context. *American Sociological Review, 61* (6), 951-972.

Bodenhausen, G. V. (2005). The role of stereotypes in decision-making processes. *Medical Decision Making, 25* (1), 112-119.

Bodenhausen, G. V. & Wyer, R. S. (1985). Effects of stereotypes on decision making and information-processing strategies. *Personality and Social Psychology, 48,* 267-282.

Bohm, R. (1991). American death penalty opinion, 1936-1986: A critical examination of the Gallup Polls. In R. Bohm (ed.), *The death penalty in America: Current research, (pp. 113-145).* Cincinnati, OH: Anderson Publishing.

Bongkoo, L., & Shafer, S. (2002). The dynamic nature of leisure experience: An application of affect control theory. *Journal of Leisure Research, 34* (3), 290-311.

Braman, A. C., & Lambert, A. J. (2001). Punishing individuals for their infirmities: Effects of personal responsibility, just-world beliefs, and in-group/out-group status. *Journal of Applied Psychology, 31,* 1095-1109.

Brennan, L. (2006, Dec. 13). New jury selection standards are designed to root out juror bias. *New Jersey Law Journal.* Retrieved March 18, 2007 from *Expanded Academic ASAP.* Thomson Gale.

Brinson, J. A., & Morris, J. R. (2001). Blacks' and Whites' perceptions of real-life scenarios: A preliminary investigation. *Journal of Humanistic Counseling, Education, and Development, 40* (2), 132-140.

Broeder, D. W. (1959). The university of Chicago jury project. *Nebraska Law Review, (38),* 744-748

Bronson, G. (1987). Focus groups for lawyers: Mock jury trials. *Forbes, 140,* 148-149.

Bureau of Justice Statistics. (2002a). Characteristics of state prison inmates. Washington, D.C.: U.S. Department of Justice. Retrieved Feb. 15, 2004 from http://www.ojp.usdoj.gov/bjs/prisons.htm.

Bureau of Justice Statistics. (2002b). Characteristics of state prison inmates. Washington, D.C.: U.S. Department of Justice. Retrieved Feb. 15, 2004 from http://www.ojp.usdoj.gov/bjs/prisons.htm.

Bureau of Justice Statistics. (2002c). Comparing federal and state inmates. Washington, D.C.: U.S. Department of Justice. Retrieved Feb. 15, 2004 from http://www.ojp.usdoj.gov/bjs/crimoff.htm#feds.

Bureau of Justice Statistics. (2002d). Federal prison population increases a record amount, state and local inmate growth moderates. Washington, D.C.: U.S. Department of Justice. Retrieved Feb. 15, 2004 from http://www.ojp.usdoj.gov/bjs/welcome.html.

Bureau of Justice Statistics. (2002e). Lifetime likelihood of going to state of federal prison. Washington, D.C.: U.S. Department of Justice. Retrieved Feb. 15, 2004 from http://www.ojp.usdoj.gov/bjs/abstract/llgsfp.htm.

Bureau of Justice Statistics (2006). Criminal offender statistics. Washington, D.C.: U.S. Department of Justice. Retrieved Feb. 9, 2007 from http://www.ojp.usdoj.gov/bjs/crimoff.htm#lifetime.

Burton Jr., V. S., Ju, X., Dunaway, G. R., & Wolfe, N. T. (1991). The correctional orientation of Bermuda prison guards: An assessment of attitudes toward punishment and rehabilitation. *International Journal of Comparative and Applied Criminal Justice, 15,* 71-80.

Calkins, B. J. (1995). Advancing psychology in the public interest: A psychologist's guide to participation in Federal advocacy process. American Psychological Association. Retrieved March 4, 2007 from http://www.apa.org/ppo/ppan/piguide.html.

Camp, D. A. (1994). Incarceration rates by race. *Journal of the Oklahoma Criminal Justice Research Consortium, 1,* 117-124.

Campbell, D., & Marable, M. (1996). Racism and schools. In D. Campbell (Ed.), *Choosing democracy: A practical guide to multicultural education (*pp. 45-79). Columbus, OH: Prentice Hall.

Carmona, L., Gorman, S., Neal, J., & Bollmer, J. (1998). Just world hypothesis. Retrieved March 10, 2007 from http://www.units.muohio.edu/psybersite/justworld/index.shtml.

Clark, K. B. (1972). Cultural deprivation theories: Their social and psychological implications. In K. B. Clark, M. Deutsch, A. Gartner, F. Keppel, H. Lewis, T. Pettigrew, L. Plotkin, & F. Riessman (Eds). *The educationally deprived: The potential for change*, (pp. 3-12). New York: Metropolitan Applied Research Center.

Cloward, R. A., & Ohlin, L. E. (1960). *Delinquency and opportunity.* New York: Free Press.

Cohen, A. K. (1955). *Delinquent boys.* New York: Free Press.

Colin, S. A. J., & Preciphs, T. K. (1991). Perceptual patterns and the learning environment: Confronting White racism. In R. Hiemstra (Ed.), *Creating environments for effective adult learning: New directions for adult and continuing education* (pp. 61-70). San Francisco: Jossey-Bass.

Cose, E. (1999, Sept. 6). The casualties of war: Using prisons to solve the drug problem hurts not just the Black and Latino communities that have suffered the most, but all of America. *Newsweek*, 29.

Coyle, M. (2002, May). Race and class penalties in crack cocaine sentencing. Washington, DC: The Sentencing Project. Retrieved Feb. 15, 2004 from http://www.sentencingproject.org/pdfs/5077.pdf.

Crack cocaine sentencing policy: Unjustified and unreasonable. (1995). Washington, D.C.: The Sentencing Project. Retrieved Feb. 15, 2004 from http://www.sentencingproject.org/pdfs/1003.pdf.

Crawford, C. (2000). Gender, race, and habitual offender sentencing in Florida. *Criminology, 38,* 263-281.

Crawford, N. (2003). American psychologists and the United Nations. *Monitor on Psychology, 34*(8), 44.

Criminal Offender Statistics (2006). Retrieved Feb. 21, 2007 from http://www.ojp.usdoj.gov/bjs/crimoff.htm.

Crocker, J., Luhtanen, R., Blaine, B., & Broadnax, S. (1994). Collective self-esteem and psychological well-being among White, Black, and Asian college students. *Personality and Social Psychology Bulletin, 20* (5), 503-513.

Crozier, S., & Joseph, S. (1997). Religiosity and sphere-specific just world beliefs in 16 to 18 year olds. *The Journal of Social Psychology, 137* (4), 510-514.

Cullen, F. T., Cullen, J. B., & Wozniak, J. F. (1988). Is rehabilitation dead? The myth of the punitive public. *Journal of Criminal Justice, 16* 303-317.

Cullen, F. T., Lutze, F. E. Link, B. G., & Wolfe, N. T. (1989). The correctional orientation of prison guards: Do officers support rehabilitation? *Federal Probation, 53,* 34-41.

Dalbert, C. (2001). A just and an unjust world: Structure and validity of different world beliefs. *Personality and Individual Differences, 30,* 561-565.

D'Alemberte, T. (1992). Racial injustice and American justice. *American Bar Association Journal, 78*, 58-60.

Dane, F. C., & Wrightsman, L. S. (1982). Effects of defendants' and victims' characteristics on jurors' verdicts. In N. L. Kerr & R. M. Bray. (Eds.), *The psychology of the courtroom* (pp. 38-54). San Diego, CA: Academic Press.

Davies, S. L. (2003). Study habits: Probing modern attempts to assess minority offender disproportionality. *Law and Contemporary Problems 66* (3), 17-49.

DeFronzo, J. (1997). Welfare and homicide. *Journal of Research in Crime and Delinquency, 34* (3), 395-407.

Diggory, J. C. (1953). Sex differences in the organization of attitudes. *Journal of Personality 22,* 89-200.

Doane, A. W. Jr. (1997). Dominant group ethnic identity in the United States: The role of "hidden" ethnicity in intergroup relations. *The Sociological Quarterly, 38* (3), 375-398.

Does the punishment fit the crime? Drug users and drunk drivers: Questions of race and class. (1993). Washington, D.C.: The Sentencing Project. Retrieved Feb. 15, 2004 from http://www.sentencingproject.org/pdfs/9040smy.pdf.

Down, W. R., Robertson, J. F., & Harrison, L. R. (1997). Control theory, labeling theory, and the delivery of services for drug abuse to adolescents. *Adolescence, 32,* 1-24.

Drug policy and the criminal justice system. (2007). Washington, D.C.: The Sentencing Project. Retrieved online Feb. 21, 2007 from: http://www.sentencingproject.org/pdfs/5047.pdf.

Durm, M. W., & Stowers, D. A. (1998). Just world beliefs and irrational beliefs: A sex difference? *Psychological Reports, 83,* 328-330.

Edwards, K. A. (2000). Stigmatizing the stigmatized: A note on the mentally ill prison inmate. *International Journal of Offender Therapy and Comparative Criminology 44*(4), 480-489.

Eisenman, R. & Dantzker, M. L. (2006). Gender and ethnic differences in sexual attitudes at a Hispanic American-serving university. *The Journal of General Psychology, 133* (2), 153-163.

Enomoto, C. E. (1999). Public sympathy for O. J. Simpson: The roles of race, age, gender, income, and education. *American Journal of Economics and Sociology, 58* (1), 145-161.

Ericson, R. V. (1977). Social distance and reaction to criminality. *British Journal of Criminality 17*(1), 16-29.

Ertel, K. (2005). Texas juror-bias decision troubles plaintiff lawyers. *Trial, 41* (6), 68-71.

Facts about prisoners and prisons. (2007). Washington, D.C.: The Sentencing Project. Retrieved Feb. 9, 2007 from http://www.sentencingproject.org/brief/pub1035.pdf.

Farkas, M. A. (1999). Correctional officer attitudes toward inmates and working with inmates in a "get tough" era. *Journal of Criminal Justice, 27,* 495-506.

Farmer, A., & Pecorino, P. (2000). Does jury bias matter? *International Review of Law and Economics, 20,* 315-328.

Farnum, R. (1997). Elite college discrimination and the limits of conflict theory. *Harvard Educational Review, 67,* 507-530.

Federal Crack Cocaine Sentencing. (2007, Feb). Retrieved Feb. 9, 2007 from http://www.sentencingproject.org/Admin/Documents/publications/dp_cracksentencing.pdf.

Ferguson, L. W. (1944a). A revision of the Primary Social Attitude Scale. *Journal of Psychology, 17,* 229-241.

Ferguson, L. W. (1944b). Socio-psychological correlates of primary attitude scales. *Journal of Social Psychology, 19,* 18-98.

Ferguson, N. (2000). The impact of sectarian injustice and the paramilitary ceasefires on adolescent just world beliefs in Northern Ireland. *The Irish Journal of Psychology, 21,* 70-77.

Finamore, P., & Carlson, J. M. (1987). Religiosity, belief in a just world and crime control attitudes. *Psychological Reports, 61,* 135-138.

Finch, B. K. (2001). Nation of origin, gender, and neighborhood differences in past-year substance use among Hispanic Americans and non-Hispanic American Whites. *Journal of Behavioral Sciences, 23* (11), 88.

Finckenauer, J. (1988). Public support for the death penalty: Retribution as just deserts or retribution as revenge? *Justice Quarterly, 5,* 81-100.

Frazier, C. E. (1978). Initial cause and societal reaction theory. *International Journal of Contemporary Sociology 15* (3), 397-413.

Free, M. D. Jr. (1997). The impact of federal sentencing reforms on African Americans. *Journal of African American Studies, 28* (2), 268-287.

Furnham, A. (1991a). A cross-cultural comparison of British and Japanese Protestant work ethic and just world beliefs. *Psychologia, 34* (1), 1-17.

Furnham, A. (1991b). Just world beliefs in twelve societies. *The Journal of Social Psychology, 133,* 317-329.

Furnham, A. (1992). Sphere-specific just world beliefs and attitudes to AIDS. *Human Relations, 45*(3), 265-268.

Furnham, A. (1995). Health, just world beliefs and coping style preferences in patients of complementary and orthodox medicine. *Social Science and Medicine, 40,* 1425-1435.

Furnham, A. (1998). Measuring the beliefs in a just world. In L. Montada & M. J. Lerner (Eds.) *Responses to victimizations and belief in a just world,* (pp. 141-162). New York: Plenum Press.

Furnham, A. (2003). Belief in a just world: Research progress over the past decade. *Personality and Individual Differences, 34,* 795-817.

Furnham, A., & Boston, N. (1996). Theories of rape and the just world. *Psychology, Crime and Law, 2,* 211-229.

Furnham, A., & Proctor, E. (1989). Belief in a just world: Review and critique of the individual difference literature. *British Journal of Social Psychology, 28,* 365-384.

Garraty, J. A. (1996). *The American nation: A history of the United States,* 5th *ed.* New York: Harper & Row.

Gastwirth, J. L., & Nayak, T. K. (1997). Statistical aspects of cases concerning racial discrimination in drug sentencing: Stephens v. State and U.S. v. Armstrong. *Journal of Criminal Law and Criminology, 87*(2), 583-603.

Gelso, C., & Fretz, B. (2001). *Counseling psychology,* 2nd ed. Fort Worth, TX: Harcourt College Publishers.

Gillmore, M. R., Catalano, R. F., Morrison, D. M., Wells, E. A., Iritani, B., & Hawkins, J. D. (1990). Racial differences in acceptability and availability of drugs and early initiation of substance use. *American Journal of Drug and Alcohol Use, 16* (3-4), 185-207.

Giordano, P. C., Cernkovich, S. A., & Rudolph, J. L. (2002). Gender, crime, and desistance: Toward a theory of cognitive transformation. *The American Journal of Sociology, 107* (4), 990-1066.

Glasser, I. (2000). American drug laws: The new Jim Crow. *Albany Law Review, 63* (3), 703.

Glasser, J. (2000, May 8). And justice for some: Minority kids are treated more harshly by the law. *U.S. News and World Report.* Retrieved March 30, 2004 from http://www.usnews.com/usnews/news/articles/000508/archive_017588.htm.

Glennon, F. (1993). Just world beliefs, self-esteem, and attitudes towards homosexuals with AIDS. *Psychological Reports, 72* (2), 584-586.

Glennon, F., Joseph, S., & Hunter, J. A. (1993). Just world beliefs in unjust societies: Northern Ireland. *The Journal of Social Psychology, 133* (4), 591-593.

Goodman, L. A., Liang, B., Helms, J. E., Latta, R. E., Sparks, E., & Weintraub, S. R. (2004). Training counseling psychologists as social justice agents: Feminist and multicultural principles in action. *The Counseling Psychologist, 32* (6), 793-837.

Gordon, R. A. (1990). Attributions for blue-collar and white-collar crime: The effects of subject and defendant race on simulated juror decisions. *Journal of Applied Social Psychology, 20,* 971-983.

Gordon, R. A., Bindrim, T. A., McNicholas, M. L., & Walden, T. L. (1988).Perceptions of blue-collar and white-collar crime: The effect of defendant race on simulated juror decisions. *The Journal of Social Psychology, 128,* 91-197.

Green, D. P., Srolovitch, D. Z., & Wong, J. S. (1998). Defended neighborhoods, integration, and racially motivated crime. *American Journal of Sociology, 104* (2), 372-403.

Greenfield, L. A., & Smith, S. K. (1999). American Indians and crime. Bureau of Justice Statistics. Retrieved Feb. 15, 2004 from http://www.ojp.usdoj.gov/bjs/pub/pdf/aic.pdf.

Hafemeister, T. L. (2000). Supreme court examines impact of errors in detecting bias during jury selection. *Violence and Victims,* 15, 209-224.

Hafer, C. (1993). Beliefs in a just world, discontent, and assertive actions by working women, *Personality and Social Psychology Bulletin, 19* (1), 30.

Hafer, C. L., & Correy, B. L. (1999). Mediators of the relation between beliefs in a just world and emotional responses to negative outcomes. *Social Justice Research, 12*(3), 189-204.

Hafer, C. L., & Olson, J. M. (1998). Individual differences in the belief in a just world and responses to personal misfortune. In L. Montada and M. J. Lerner (Eds.) *Responses to victimizations and belief in a just world,* (pp. 65-86). New York: Plenum Press.

Hansman, C. A., Spencer, L. E., & Grant, D. (1999). Beyond diversity: Dismantling barriers in education. *Journal of Instructional Psychology, 26,* 16-21.

Headley, S. (2003). Labeling and delinquency. *Youth Studies Australia, 22* (4), 61-62.

Heaney, G. (1991). The reality of guidelines sentencing: No end to disparity. *American Criminal Law Review, 28,* 161-232.

Herrnstein, R. J., & Murray, C. (1994). *The bell curve: Intelligence and class structure in American life.* New York: Simon & Schuster.

Hillier, L., & Foddy, M. (1993). The role of observable attitudes in judgments of blame in cases of wife assault. *Sex Roles: A Journal of Research, 29* (9), 629-645.

Hirschi, T. (1969). *The causes of delinquency.* Berkeley, CA: The University of California Press.

Hispanic Americans in the United States (2007, March). Retrieved March 6, 2007 from http://en.wikipedia.org/wiki/Hispanic_American.

Holcomb-McCoy, C. (2005). Ethnic identity development in early adolescence: implications and recommendations for middle school counselors. *Professional School Counseling* 9 (2), 120-128.

Holloway, M. (1999, Jan). Flynns' effect. *Scientific American,* 37-38.

Hunt, M. O. (2000). Status, religion, and the belief in a just world: Comparing African Americans, Latinos, and Whites. *Social Science Quarterly, 81* (1), 325-345.

Hurwitz, J., & Peffley, M. (1997). Public perceptions of race and crime: The role of racial stereotypes. *American Journal of Political Sciences, 41* (2), 375-401.

Inciardi, J. A. (1972). Visibility, societal reaction, and criminal behavior. *Criminology, 10* (2), 217-233.

International Center for Prison Studies (2007). Retrieved March 3, 2007 from http://www.kcl.ac.uk/depsta/rel/icps/worldbrief/highest_to_lowest_rates.php.

Jackson, J. E., & Ammen, S. (1996). Race and correctional officers' punitive attitudes toward treatment programs for inmates. *Journal of Criminal Justice, 24* (2), 153-167.

Jensen, A. R. (1967). The culturally disadvantaged: Psychological and educational aspects. *Educational Research, 10,* 4-20.

Jensen. A. R. (1969a). How much can we boost IQ and scholastic achievement? *Harvard Educational Letter, 39* (1), 1-123.

Jensen, A. R. (1969b). Jensen's theory of intelligence: A reply. *Journal of Educational Psychology, 60,* 427-431.

Jensen, A. R. (1969c). Race and intelligence: The differences are real. *Psychology Today, 3,* 4-6.

Jensen, A. R. (1970). Race and the genetics of intelligence: A reply to Lewontin. *Bulletin of the Atomic Scientists, 26,* 17-23.

Jensen, A. R. (1972). IQ and race: Ethical issues. *The Humanist, 32,* 4-6.

Johnson, J. D., Simmons, C. H., Jordon, A., MacLean, L., Taddel, J., & Thomas, D. (2002). Rodney King and O. J. revisited: The impact of race and defendant empathy induction on judicial decisions. *Journal of Applied Social Psychology, 32* (6), 1208-1223.

Jones, D. S. (2006). Racial profiling in psychiatry: Does it help patients? *Psychiatric Times, 23* (14), 43-53.

Joseph, S., & Stringer, M. S. (1998). Just world beliefs in Northern Ireland. *The Journal of Social Psychology, 138,* 263-267.

Jurand, S. H. (2001). Juror studies show bias, discontent. *Trial, 37* (1), 94.

Jurand, S. H. (2003). European ethnic groups win protection from bias in jury selection. *Trial, 39* (12), 80-81.

Kaiser, F. (2003). Two challenges to a moral extension of the theory of planned behavior: Moral norms and just world beliefs in conservationism. *Personality and Individual Differences, 35,* 1033-1038.

Kane, E. W. (2000, Annual). Racial and ethnic variations in gender-related attitudes. *Annual Review of Sociology,* 419.

Kaukinen, C., & Colavecchia, S. (1999). Public perceptions of the courts: An examination of attitudes toward the treatment of victims and accused. *Canadian Journal of Criminology, 41* (3), 365-384.

Kershaw, T. (1997). The effects of mood on just world beliefs and attitudes toward a victim. Unpublished Master's Thesis, Wayne State University, Detroit Michigan.

Kim, B. S. K., & Abreu, J. M. (2001). Acculturation measurement: Theory, current instruments, and future directions. In J. G. Ponterotto, J. M. Casas, L. A. Suzuki, & C. M. Alexander (Eds.) *Handbook of multicultural counseling,* 2nd ed, (pp. 394-424). Thousand Oaks, CA: Sage Publishing.

King, N. J. (1993). Postconviction review of jury discrimination: Measuring the effects of juror race on jury decisions. *Michigan Law Review, 92* (1), 63-130.

King, R. S., & Mauer, M. (2002, Sept). Distorted priorities: Drug offenders in state prisons. Washington, D.C.: The Sentencing Project. Retrieved Feb. 15, 2004 from http://www.sentencingproject.org/pdfs/9038.pdf.

Kiselica, M. S., & Robinson, M. (2001). Bringing advocacy counseling to life: The history, issues, and human dramas of social justice work in counseling. *Journal of Counseling and Development, 79,* 387-397.

Klofas, J. M., & Toch, H. (1982). The guard subculture myth. *Journal of Research in Crime and Delinquency, 19,* 238-254.

Kohn, S. (1995). Dismantling sociocultural barriers to care. *The Healthcare Forum Journal, 38* (3), 30.

Kristiansen, C. (1990). Perceptions of wife abuse: Effects of gender, attitudes toward women, and just world beliefs among college students. *Psychology of Women Quarterly, 14,* 177-179.

Lambert, A. J. (1999). Perceptions of risk and the buffering process: The role of just world beliefs and right-wing authoritarianism. *Personality and Social Psychology Bulletin, 25,* 643-649.

Lambert, A. J., Burroughs, T., & Nguyen, T. (1999). Perceptions of risk and the "buffering hypothesis:" The role of just world beliefs and right-wing authoritarianism. *Personality and Social Psychology Bulletin, 25*, 643-656.

Lambert, A. J., & Raichle, K. (2000). The role of political ideology in mediating judgments of blame in rape victims and their assailants: A test of the just world, personal responsibility and legitimization hypotheses. *Personality and Social Psychology Bulletin, 26* (7), 853-863.

Landwehr, P. H., Bothwell, R. K., Jeanmard, M., Luque, L. R., Brown, R. L., & Breaux, M. A. (2002). Racism in rape trials. *The Journal of Social Psychology, 142* (5), 667-671.

Las Cruces, New Mexico (2007). Retrieved March 6, 2007 from http://www.city-data.com/city/Las-Cruces-New-Mexico.html.

Leiber, M. J., & Woodrick, A. C. (1997). Religious beliefs, attributional styles, and adherence to correctional orientations. *Criminal Justice and Behavior, 24* (4), 495-511.

Lerner, M. J. (1977). The justice motive. Some hypotheses as to its origins and forms. *Journal of Personality, 45,* 1-52.

Lerner, M. J. (1980). *The belief in a just world: A fundamental delusion.* New York: Plenum.

Lerner, M. J. (1998). The two forms of belief in a just world: Some thoughts on why and how people care about justice. In L. Montada & M. J. Lerner (Eds.). *Responses to victimization and belief in a just world, (*pp. 247-269). New York: Plenum Press.

Lerner, M. J., & Miller, D. T. (1978). Just world research and the attribution process: Looking back and ahead. *Psychological Bulletin, 85* (5), 1030-1051.

Lerner, M. J., & Montada, L. (1998). An overview: Advances in belief in a just world theory and methods. In L. Montada & M. J. Lerner (Eds.) *Responses to victimizations and belief in a just world.* (pp. 1-7). New York, NY: Plenum Press.

Levin, D. J., Langan, P. A., & Brown, J. M. (2000, Feb). State court sentencing of convicted felons, 1996. U.S. Department of Justice Statistics, Bureau of Justice Statistics, (pp. 8-20). Retrieved Feb. 15, 2004 from http://www.ojp.usdoj.gov/bjs/abstract/scscfst.htm.

Lillie-Blanton, M., Anthony, J. C., & Schuster, C. R. (1993). Probing the meaning of racial/ethnic group comparisons in crack cocaine smoking. *The Journal of the American Medical Association, 269* (80), 993-998.

Lilly, J. R., Cullen, F. T., & Ball, R. A. (1989). *Criminological theory: Context and consequences.* Newbury Park, CA: Sage Publications.

Lipkus, I. M., & Bissonnette, V. L. (1996). Relationships among belief in a just world, willingness to accommodate, and marital well-being. *Personality and Social Psychology Bulletin, 22,* 1043-1056.

Lipkus, I. M., Dalbert, C., & Siegler, I. C. (1996). The importance of distinguishing the belief in a just world for self versus others: Implications for psychological well-being. *Personality and Social Psychology Bulletin, 22,* 666-677.

Lipkus, I. M., & Siegler, I. C. (1993). The belief in a just world and perceptions of discrimination. *Journal of Psychology, 127* (4), 465-474.

Liska, A. E., & Yu, J. (1992). Specifying and testing the threat hypothesis: Police use of deadly force. In A. E. Liska (ed). *Social threat and social control* (pp. 48-55). Albany, NY: State University of New York.

Lorge, I. (1939). The Thurstone attitude scales: Reliability and consistency of rejection and acceptance. *Journal of Social Psychology, 10* 187-198.

Luna, E. (2003). Race, crime, and institutional design. *Law and Contemporary Problems, 66* (3), 183-221.

MacCoun, R. J. (1989). Experimental research on jury decision-making. *Science, 244*, 1046-1051.

Maes, J. (1998a). Eight stages in the development of research on the construct of belief in a just world. In L. Montada, & M. J. Lerner (Eds.) *Responses to victimizations and belief in a just world,* (pp. 163-185). New York: Plenum Press.

Maes, J. (1998b). Immanent justice and ultimate justice: Two ways of believing in justice. In L. Montada, & M. J. Lerner (Eds.) *Responses to victimizations and belief in a just world,* (pp. 9-41). New York: Plenum Press.

Mahar, D. (2001). Positioning in a middle school culture: Gender, race, social class, and power: Adolescent discourse patterns outside of school can illuminate the stance of students in the classroom. *Journal of Adolescent and Adult Literacy, 45* (3), 200-210.

Malik, K. (1996, Sept. 6). No platform, or no democracy? *New Statesman,* 14-15.

Matthews, F. L. (2000). Incarceration, higher education and hypocrisy. *African American Issues in Higher Education, 17* (6), 6.

Mauer, M. (2001). *Race to incarcerate.* New York, NY: New Press.

Mauer, M. (2003). Invisible punishment block housing, education, voting. Joint Center for Political and Economic Studies. Retrieved March 22, 2005 from http://www.sentencingproject.org/pdfs/mauer-focus.pdf.

Mauer, M., & Chesney-Lind, M. (2003). *Invisible punishment: The collateral consequences of mass imprisonment.* New York, NY: New Press.

Mauro, T. (2005, June 20). High court invokes Batson in two jury bias cases. *New Jersey Law Journal,* p. NA. Retrieved March 18, 2007 from *Expanded Academic ASAP.* Thomson Gale.

Mazella, R., & Feingold, A. (1994). The effects of physical attractiveness, race, socioeconomic status, and gender of defendants and victims on judgments of mock jurors: A meta-analysis. *Journal of Applied Social Psychology, 24,* 1315-1344.

McDonald, D., & Carlson, K. (1993). Sentencing in the federal courts: Does race matter? The transition to sentencing guidelines, 1986-90 (Summary) (U.S. Department of Justice, Bureau of Justice Statistics). Washington, D.C.: US Government Printing Office.

McGoldrick, M., Giordano, J., & Pearch, J. K. (1996). *Ethnicity and family therapy, 2nd ed.* New York: Guilford Press.

McIntosh, P. (1989, July/Aug). White privilege: Unpacking the invisible knapsack. *Peace and Freedom,* 10-12.

Melvin, K. B., Gramling, L. K., & Gardner, W. M. (1985). A scale to measure attitudes toward prisoners. *Criminal Justice and Behavior, 12,* 241-253.

Merton, R. (1938). Social structure and anomie. *American Sociological Review, 3,* 672-682.

Miller, D. C. (1983). *Handbook of research design and social measurement, 4th ed.* New York: Longman.

Miller, M., & Hewitt, J. (1978). Conviction of a defendant as juror-victim racial similarity. *The Journal of Social Psychology, 105,* 159-160.

Mohr, P. B., & Luscri, G. (1995). Social work orientation and just world beliefs. *The Journal of Social Psychology, 135,* 101-104.

Montada, L. (1998). Belief in a just world : A hybrid of justice motive and self-interest. In L. Montada, & M. J. Lerner (Eds.) *Responses to victimizations and belief in a just world,* (pp. 217-247). New York: Plenum Press.

Moran, G., Cutler, B. L., & De Lisa, A. (1994). Attitudes toward tort reform, scientific jury selection, and juror bias : Verdict inclination in criminal and civil trials. *Law and Psychology Review, 18,* 309-326.

Morgan, R. D., Beer A. M., Fitzgerald, K. L., & Mandracchia, J. T. (2007). Graduate students' experiences, interests, and attitudes toward correctional/forensic psychology. *Criminal Justice and Behavior,* 34 (96), 96-108.

Morgan, R. D., Rozycki, A. T., & Wilson, S. (2004). Inmate perceptions of mental health services. *Professional Psychology: Research and Practice, 35*, 389-396.

Murray, C. B., Kaiser, R., & Taylor, S. (1997). The O. J. Simpson verdict: Predictors of beliefs about innocence or guilt. *Journal of Social Sciences, 53* (3), 455-476.

Murray, J. D., Spadafore, J. A., & McIntosh, W. D. (2005). Belief in a just world and social perception: Evidence for automatic activation. *The Journal of Social Psychology, 145* (1), 35-49.

Mwamwenda, T. S. (1999). Gender differences in attitudes toward wife battering. *The Journal of Social Psychology, 139* (6), 790.

Na, E., & Loftus, E. F. (1998). Attitudes toward law and prisoners, conservative authoritarianism, attribution, and internal-external locus of control. *Journal of Cross-Cultural Psychology, 29* (5), 595-616.

Nelson, S. A. (1992). Effects of forced sexual contact and childhood emotional, physical, and sexual abuse on just world beliefs and hostility. Unpublished Master's Thesis: University of Wyoming, Laramie, Wyoming.

New incarceration figures: Thirty-three consecutive years of growth. (Dec. 2006). The Sentencing Project. Retrieved March 3, 2007 from http://www.sentencingproject.org/PublicationDetails.aspx?PublicationID=430.

New Mexico criminal and traffic law manual. (2004). Reprinted from the Michie's Annotated Statutes of New Mexico and 2004 Cumulative Supplement. Lexis Nexis.

New York study finds that minority defendants are given harsher sentences than Whites. (1996). *Jet, 89* (24), 38.

Nielsen, L. B. (2000). Situating legal consciousness: Experiences and attitudes of ordinary citizens about law and street harassment. *Law and Society Review, 34* (4), 1055-1090.

Ogletree, A. (2006). The literature of immigration and racial formation: Becoming White, becoming other, becoming American in the late progressive era. *Journal of Ethnic and Migration Studies, 32* (4), 741-743.

Oliver, J. E., & Mendelberg, T. (2000). Reconsidering the environmental determinants of White racial attitudes. *American Journal of Political Science, 44* (3), 574-589.

Olson, E. (2000, May 18). Geneva panel says U.S. prisoner restraints amount to torture. New York Times.

Oppenheimer, G. M. (2001). Paradigm lost: Race, ethnicity, and the search for a new population taxonomy. *American Journal of Community Psychology, 17,* 17-31.

O'Quin, K., & Vogler, C. C. (1989). Effects of just world beliefs on perceptions of crime perpetrators and victims. *Social Justice Research, 3* (1), 47-56.

Pedraza, S., & Rumbaut, R. G. (1996). *Origins and destinies: Immigration, race, and ethnicity in America.* Boston, MA: Wadsworth.

Perdue, J. M. (2005). Tips for weeding out juror bias. *Trial, 41* (7), 54-60.

Peretz and Black mothers (1994, April 25). *The Nation,* 548.

Petersilia, J. (1983). Racial disparities in the criminal justice system: Prepared for the National Institute of Corrections, U.S. Department of Justice. Santa Monica, CA: Rand.

Platt, A. M. (2001). Social insecurity: The transformation of American criminal justice, 1965-2000. *Social Justice, 28* (1), 138-155.

Pruitt, L. P. (2002). Overcoming jury bias. *Defense Counsel Journal,* 69 (3), 331-339.

Quillian, L. (1995). Prejudice as a response to perceived group threat: Population composition and anti-immigrant and racial prejudice in Europe. *American Sociological Review, 60* (4), 586-611.

Radelet, M. L. (1995, March-April). Race and death. *Index on Censorship, 124-126.*

Redfield, R., Linton, R., & Herskovits, M. J. (1936). Memorandum on the study of acculturation. *American Anthropologist, 56,* 973-1002.

Reducing racial disparity in the criminal justice system. (2002) Washington, D.C.: The Sentencing Project. Retrieved online Aug. 15, 2003 from: http://www.sentencingproject.org/pdfs/5079.pdf.

Reducing racial disparity in the criminal justice system. (2007). Washington, D.C.: The Sentencing Project. Retrieved online Feb. 9, 2007 from: http://www.sentencingproject.org/pdfs/5079.pdf.

Report finds racial disparities in Seattle drug arrests. (2003, Dec. 15). *Alcoholism & Drug Abuse Weekly,* 8.

Robinson, D., Porporino, F. J., & Simourd, L. (1993). The influence of career orientation on support for rehabilitation among correctional staff. *The Prison Journal, 73,* 162-177.

Robinson, D. T., Smith-Lovin, L., & Tsoudis, O. (1994). Heinous crime or unfortunate accident? The effects of remorse on responses to mock criminal confessions. *Social Forces, 73* (1), 175-191.

Romero, D. & Chan, A. (2005). Profiling Derald Wing Sue: Blazing the trail for the multicultural journey and social justice in counseling. *Journal of Counseling and Development, 83,* 202-213.

Rosenfield, S. (1997). The effects of received services and perceived stigma on life satisfaction. *American Sociological Review, 62* (4), 660-672.

Rubin, Z., & Peplau, L. A. (1975). Who believes in a just world? *Journal of Social Issues, 31,* 65-89.

Rutledge, D. M. (1995). Social Darwinism, scientific racism, and the metaphysics of race. *Journal of Negro Education, 64* (3), 243-252.

Schmitt, E. L., Langan, P. A., & Durose, M. R. (2002). Characteristics of drivers stopped by police in 1999. Bureau of Justice Statistics. Retrieved Mar. 4, 2004 from http://www.ojp.usdoj.gov/bjs/pub/pdf/cdsp99.pdf.

Schur, L. A., & Kruse, D. L. (1992). Gender differences in attitudes toward unions. *Industrial and Labor Relations Review 46* (1), 89-102.

Seligman, D. (1992). *A question of intelligence: The IQ debate in America.* New York: Birch Lane Press.

Sellers, R. M., Smith, M. A., Shelton, J. N., Rowley, S. A. J., & Chavous, T. M. (1998). Multidimensinoal model of racial identity: A reconceptualization of African American racial identity. *Personality and Social Psychology Review, 2* (1), 18-39.

Shaw, M. E., & Wright, J. M. (1967). *Scales for the measurement of attitudes.* New York: McGraw-Hill.

Simourd, L. (1997). Staff attitudes toward inmates and correctional work: An exploration of the attitude-work outcome relationship. Unpublished document, Carleton University. As cited in Teller, C., Dowden, C., Foumer, J., & Franson, J. (2001). Correctional Officers Professional Orientation Scales. Research Branch Correctional Services Canada. Retrieved Feb. 15, 2004 from: http://www.csc-scc.gc.ca/text/rsrch/reports/r103_e.pdf.

Smith, E. J. (1991). Ethnic identity development: Toward the development of a theory within the context of majority/minority status. *Journal of Counseling and Development, 70* (1), 181-188.

Smith, S. A. (1999). The "ebonics" resolution: Concepts of culture and language in the miseducation of African-American children. Unpublished Master's Thesis, Bank Street College of Education.

Sokefeld, M. (1999). Debating self, identity, and culture in anthropology. *Current Anthropology 40* (4), 417.

Sorensen, J., Hope, R., & Stemen, D. (2003). Racial disproportionality in state prison admissions: Can regional variation be explained by differential arrest rates? *Journal of Criminal Justice 31* (1), 73-85.

Sphon, C., & Holleran, D. (2000). The imprisonment penalty paid by young, unemployed, Black, and Hispanic American male offenders. *Criminology 38*, 281-307.

Steffensmeier, D., & Demuth, S. (2001). Ethnicity and judges' sentencing decisions: Hispanic – Black-White comparisons. *Criminology, 39,* 145.

Stinchcombe, A., Adams, R., Heimer, C., Scheppele, K., Smith, T., & Taylor, G. (1980). *Crime and punishment: Changing attitudes in America.* San Francisco: Jossey-Bass.

Strier, F., & Shestowsky, D. (1999). Profiling the profilers: A study of the trial consulting profession, its impact on trial justice and what, if anything, to do about it. *Wisconsin Law Review, 29,* 441-499.

Study shows justice department lawyers seek death penalty most for minorities. (1998). *Jet, 98* (17), 14.

Sue, D. W., & Sue, D. (1999). *Counseling the culturally different: Theory and practice,* 3rd ed. New York: John Wiley & Sons.

Taylor, C. M. (1981). W.E.B. DuBois's challenge to scientific racism. *Journal of African American Studies, 11* (4), 449-460.

Taylor, G., Scheppele, K., & Stinchcombe, A. (1979). Salience of crime and support for harsher criminal sanctions. *Social Problems, 26,* 413-423.

Thurstone, L. L. (1932). *The measurement of social attitudes.* Chicago: University of Chicago Press.

Tomes, H. (2004). The case and the research that forever connected psychology with policy. *Monitor on Psychology, 35* (6), 28.

Turner, C. (1996). What's the story? An analysis of juror discrimination and a plea for affirmative jury selection. *American Criminal Law Review, 34* (1), 289-323.

Uebel, T. E. (1990). Scientific racism in the philosophy of science: Some historical examples. *The Philosophical Forum, XXII* (1), 1-18.

Ugwuegbu, D. C. (1979). Racial and evidential factors in juror attribution of legal responsibility. *Journal of Experimental Social Psychology, 15,* 133-146.

Unnever, J. D., Frazier, C. E., & Henretta, J. C. (1980). Race differences in criminal sentences. *The Sociological Quarterly, 21,* 197-205.

U.S. Census Bureau Quick Facts. (2005). Retrieved Feb. 10, 2007 from http://quickfacts.census.gov/qfd/states/53000.html.

U.S. Sentencing Commission (1991). The federal sentencing guidelines: A report on the operation of the guidelines system and short-term impact on disparity in sentencing, use of incarceration, and prosecutorial discretion and plea bargaining (Vol. 2). Washington, D.C.: Author.

Valk, A., & Karu, K. (2001). Ethnic attitudes in relation to ethnic pride and ethnic differentiation. *Journal of Social Psychology, 141* (5), 583-602.

Vera, E. M. & Speight, S. L. (2003). Multicultural competence, social justice, and counseling psychology: Expanding our roles. *The Counseling Psychologist, 31* (3), 253-272.

Verkuyten, M. (2003). Ethnic in-group bias among minority and majority early adolescents: The perception of negative peer behavior. *British Journal of Developmental Psychology, 21* (4), 543-564.

Walker, B. W. (2007). Counter jury bias in your opening. *Trial,* 43 (2), 70-73.

Webster, M. (1993). *Merriam Webster's collegiate dictionary, 10th ed.* Merriam-Webster, Inc: Springfield, MA

Whitehead, J. T., & Lindquist, C. A. (1992). Determinants of probation and parole officer professional orientation. *Journal of Criminal Justice, 20,* 13-24.

Williams, J. J. (1995). Race of appellant, sentencing guidelines, and decision making in criminal appeals: A research note. *Journal of Criminal Justice, 38* (4), 439-467.

Wortley, S. (1996). Justice for all? Race and perception of bias in the Ontario criminal justice system—A Toronto survey. *Canadian Journal of Criminology, 38* (4), 439-467.

Wuensch, K. L., Campbell, M. W., Kesler, F. C., & Moore, C. H. (2002). Racial bias in decisions made by mock jurors evaluating a case of sexual harassment. *The Journal of Social Psychology, 142* (5), 587-601.

Yueh-Ting, L., & Ottati, V. (2002). Attitudes toward U.S. immigration policy: The roles of in-group—out-group bias, economic concern, and obedience to law. *The Journal of Social Psychology, 142* (5), 617-635.

CPSIA information can be obtained at www.ICGtesting.com
Printed in the USA
LVOW091524290512

283767LV00004B/185/P

9 783838 373423